EIGHT PHILOSOPHICAL CLASSICS

Introductory Readings from Plato, Aristotle, Anselm of Canterbury, Thomas Aquinas, René Descartes, David Hume, Immanuel Kant, & Jean-Paul Sartre

Second Edition

Translated, Paraphrased, & Edited by

George Cronk

Harcourt Brace & Company
Orlando, Florida
1998

Custom Publisher   Joann Manos
Senior Production Manager   Sue Dunaway

Eight Philosophical Classics
Copyright © 1999 by George Cronk

Permissions Department
Harcourt Brace & Company
6277 Sea Harbor Drive
Orlando, FL 32887-6777

Printed in the United States of America

0-15-567377-7

PREFACE

This is an anthology of reader-friendly selections from eight classics in the Western philosophical tradition. The selections are partly translations and partly paraphrases. I have tried to make them faithful to the original-language texts and, at the same time, available to the reader in an idiomatic American English of the 1990s. In the few places where my translation-paraphrases deviate significantly from the original-language texts, I have footnoted this fact and have included in the footnote the actual original-language passage in question.

There are excellent standard translations of these classics into English, but some of them are quite old and thus rendered in an English of the early 20th century, and most of them were done mainly for the scholarly community and not aimed at an audience of general and introductory readers.[1] In my work on this collection, I have

---

[1]For example, see Paul Shorey's translation of Plato's *Republic* (1930) in *Plato: The Collected Dialogues*, ed. Edith Hamilton and Huntington Cairns (New York: Pantheon Books, a Division of Random House, Inc., 1961), 575-844; W.D. Ross's translation of Aristotle's *Nicomachean Ethics* (1925) in *The Complete Works of Aristotle*, ed. Jonathan Barnes (Princeton: Princeton University Press, 1984), 1279-1867; S.N. Dean's translation of Anselm's *Proslogium* (1962) in *St. Anselm: Basic Writings* (La Salle, Illinois: Open Court Publishing Company, 1962), 47-80; the translation of the *Summa Theologica* of St. Thomas Aquinas by the Fathers of the English Dominican Province (1911, revised in 1920) (Westminster, Maryland: Christian Classics, 5 vols., 1981); Donald A. Cress's translation of Descartes' *Meditations* (1980) in René Descartes, *Discourse on Method and Meditations on First Philosophy* (Indianapolis: Hackett Publishing Company, 1980), 43-100; Norman Kemp Smith's translation of Kant's *Critique of Pure Reason* (1929) (New York: St.

constantly kept before my mind an audience made up of college students and general readers who are neither professional philosophers nor philosophy majors (although I think that such majors could reap some benefit from these translations).

In addition to making the translations as readable as possible, I have, as a further aid to the reader, broken each text up into clearly-labeled sections that more or less outline the structure and major themes of the author's argument.

A special word with regard to my "translation" of the selections from David Hume's *Inquiry Concerning Human Understanding*: Hume, of course, wrote in English; but it was 18th century English. His sentences are very long (sometimes paragraph-long), his 18th century vocabulary is often unclear from the standpoint of current usage, and his punctuation can be quite confusing to the late 20th century reader. In putting this material by Hume into 1990s American English, I have reconstructed his paragraphs with shorter sentences, replaced much of his vocabulary with terminology more familiar to readers today, and modernized his punctuation. Throughout, however, I have made every effort to preserve the philosophical thrust and meaning of Hume's original text, and I hope that my efforts herein will not be regarded as sacrilege by Hume scholars and enthusiasts.[2]

Martin's Press, 1965); and Bernard Frechtman's translation of Sartre's "Existentialism" in *Existentialism and Human Emotions* (New York: Philosophical Library, 1957), 9-51.

[2]A highly regarded standard edition of Hume's *Inquiry* is *An Enquiry Concerning Human Understanding and A Letter from a Gentlemen to His Friend in Edinburgh*, ed. Eric Steinberg (Indianapolis: Hackett Publishing Company, 1977).

My dear wife and colleague, Dr. Sherida Yoder, Professor of English at Felician College, Lodi, New Jersey, read each and every selection in this anthology and recommended many changes that have made the final versions of these materials far more readable than they would have been without her able contributions.

CONTENTS

PLATO
(427-347 BC)

From the REPUBLIC[1]

The Philosopher Ruler

But . . . Socrates [said Glaucon], . . . you have digressed from our main topic -- that is, whether it is possible for the political system we have been discussing to come into existence and, if so, how . . . .

Tell me, Glaucon [said Socrates], do you think that a painter is a failure if he paints an excellent picture of an exceedingly fine and beautiful human being but can't prove that such a person could actually exist?

Not at all.

---

[1]Translated, paraphrased, and edited by George Cronk. © 1996. The *Republic* is a long work, written in classical Greek, and traditionally divided into ten "books." The present translation includes only the end of Book V (471c-480a), parts of Book VI (484a-d and 504e-511e), and the first part of Book VII (514a-521b). The reference numbers in parentheses in the preceding sentence are to the pages and sections of pages in the authoritative edition of the Greek text of Plato's writings, which was published by Henri Estienne (a/k/a Stephanus) in 1578. This is the standard scholarly convention for exact citations of passages in Plato's writings. For the Greek text, together with a standard English translation by Paul Shorey, see the bilingual edition of Plato, *The Republic*, 2 Vols. (Cambridge, MA: Harvard University Press, The Loeb Classical Library, 1937).

But didn't we agree that we were trying to develop a theoretical model of a good political system?

Yes.

Then you can't say that we are incompetent theoreticians if we can't prove that the system we are constructing in theory could actually exist.

I concede that . . . .

Well, then, you must also concede that, since theory is more exact and clear than practice, it is improbable or even impossible for an actual political system to conform exactly to our theoretical model. If we do try to prove that it is possible for a good political system to exist, it will be sufficient if the actual system comes close to the theoretical model. Will you agree to these terms?

Yes, I will.

OK. Let's start by pointing out the major flaw in currently existing and badly governed political systems and what it would take to eliminate that flaw so that an actual system could be run reasonably well . . . . What I am going to say now will seem outlandish or even absurd to many, but I think that unless a political system is ruled by philosophers, or unless those who are ruling become true philosophers -- that is, unless political power and philosophy are brought together and those who now pursue either the one or the other exclusively are prevented from doing so -- neither our political problems nor our human troubles in general can be ended . . . .

2

True philosophy and true philosophers

In order to make this apparently wild claim plausible, we had better define what we mean by a philosopher . . . . What we need to do is show that some people are naturally suited to practice philosophy and to be political leaders while most other people should stay away from philosophy and follow their leaders . . . .

Lead on [said Glaucon].

Isn't it true that, if someone really loves something, he must love that thing as a whole and not just some aspects of it?

Please explain; I don't get it . . . .

Well, haven't you noticed that men who love boys love *all* boys in the bloom of youth and not only some of them . . . ?

If you insist on asking me how lovers of boys behave, I will agree with what you have said, for the sake of the argument.

And what about wine-lovers? Don't they love *all* wines and seek every opportunity to taste them?

Yes.

And I'm sure you've seen how ambitious people, if they cannot become generals, are willing to be captains; and if they are not respected by important and powerful people, they are content to be respected by lesser people. It is status and respect in general that they want.

I have noticed that.

3

Then doesn't it follow that, when someone loves something, he loves the whole thing, and not just some parts of it?

Yes, he loves the whole thing.

Then it also follows that the philosopher (that is, the lover of wisdom) wants the whole of wisdom, not just some aspects of it, right?

Right . . . .

Therefore, those who love and pursue all kinds of learning and have a boundless appetite for it have what it takes to be philosophers....

But what [asked Glaucon] is a true philosopher?

Someone who loves the sight of truth [said Socrates].

What exactly does that mean?

It's not easy to explain it, but won't you agree that, since beauty is the opposite of the ugly, they are two different things?

Yes.

And each of them is a single thing, isn't it?

Yes.

And the same is true of the just and the unjust, the good and the bad, and all other such pairs, isn't it? Each by itself is a single thing, but each appears to be many because it shows itself in many different situations and in association with various actions, objects, and so forth. Is that correct?

Yes, it is.

Here, then, we find a major difference between true philosophers and those who are not suited for philosophy . . . . There are people -- in fact, there are *many* people -- who love beautiful sounds, colors, and shapes and who take delight in art works made up of such elements, but who are incapable of seeing and grasping the nature of the beautiful itself . . . . But there are only a few who are capable of approaching beauty in itself and seeing it as it really is. Are you following me?

Yes, I am.

Now, it seems that, of those who do not grasp the beautiful itself, some (perhaps the majority) do not even recognize the existence of beauty as such but believe only in the existence of beautiful things. Such people are also incapable of following anyone who knows how to reach an understanding of beauty itself. Don't you think that people like this are dreaming rather than being really awake, since they believe that the likenesses of a thing [instances of beauty] are the thing itself [beauty]?

I see what you mean.

Then you must agree that someone who believes in the existence of the beautiful itself and can see both it and its likenesses, and who does not confuse beauty with its likenesses, is awake rather than dreaming.

Yes, he is very much awake.

Knowledge, ignorance, and opinion

And can't we say that this person has *knowledge* [of the nature of beauty], whereas the other type of person only has *opinion* [about what things are beautiful]?

Yes, that seems right . . . .

Now, does someone who knows know something or nothing?

He knows something.

Something that exists or something that does not exist?

Something that exists. How can something that does not exist be known?

Then that which is completely real is completely knowable, and that which is completely unreal is completely unknowable. Right?

Right.

OK. Now, if there are things that are both real and unreal, they must stand between the completely real and the completely unreal. Isn't that true?

Yes.

Then if knowledge is of the real and ignorance necessarily belongs to the unreal [that is, an ignorant belief has *nothing* to support it], then there must be a state of mind midway between knowledge and ignorance, a state having to do with those things that are both real and unreal (if there are any such things)?

6

I agree.

Now, is there such a thing as *opinion*?

Of course.

And it is different from knowledge?

Yes.

And since opinion and knowledge are different, they must have different objects, right?

Right.

And we have agreed that the object of knowledge is reality . . . . But before we go further on this point, we had better get clear about something else.

What's that?

Aren't there "powers" or "abilities" that enable human beings and other creatures to do whatever they are capable of doing? I mean things like sight and hearing. Do you understand?

Yes, I do.

Well, here's something interesting. We can't distinguish one ability from another in the same way we distinguish between other things, that is, by looking at their colors, shapes, or other such characteristics, because abilities have no such perceptible qualities. We can only distinguish between abilities on the basis of what they do and what they do it to [that is, by their functions and objects] . . . . From this point of view, knowledge is an ability, isn't it?

7

Yes, it is.

And what about opinion?

It's an ability too since it enables us to form opinions.

But we agreed earlier that opinion and knowledge are not the same, right?

Right.

And each has its own end or object and its own function?

Yes.

Do we also agree that the object of knowledge is what is (reality) and that the function of the power of knowing is to know what is . . . and that the function of the power of opinion is to form opinions?

Yes.

But then what is the end or object of opinion? Is it reality, which is also the object of knowledge? Wouldn't that make the knowable and the opinionable the same? Is that possible?

No, it's impossible. If different powers or abilities have different functions and objects, and if opinion and knowledge are different powers, then they can have neither the same functions nor the same objects.

Then if the object of knowledge is what is, the object of opinion must be other than what is?

Yes.

Are opinions then about *nothing* . . . ? But haven't we agreed that *ignorance* is based on *nothing* (that which is not) and that knowledge is directed to what is?

Yes.

So it seems that the object of opinion is neither what is nor what is not . . . and that opinion is neither knowledge nor ignorance . . . . It also seems that opinion is less clear than knowledge and more clear than ignorance . . . and that it must stand between them. Do you agree with these conclusions?

Yes, I do.

What else is left to do, then? It seems that we must decide whether there is anything that is both real and unreal at the same time and that cannot be said to be either perfectly real or completely unreal. If there are such things, then they are the objects of opinion . . . . Right?

Right.

Lovers of opinion versus lovers of wisdom

Let's go back then to the people who don't believe in the existence of beauty itself . . . but who do believe in the existence of various beautiful things . . . . Let's ask such a person the following question: "My friend, of all the many beautiful things in the world, are there any that are always beautiful and never ugly, or is every beautiful thing capable of appearing ugly under certain circumstances . . . ?" How would such a person answer, Glaucon?

He would say that the things in the world that are sometimes beautiful are also ugly in some situations. They are both beautiful in a way and ugly in a way . . . .

And what about things that are large, small, light, and heavy. Can't each of them be the opposite in certain situations?

Yes, each thing can be both large and small, light and heavy. [For example, a given rock can be large relative to a smaller one and small relative to a larger one.]

So isn't it true, then, that each one of a pair of opposites no more *is* what it is said to be than it *is not* what it is said to be?

[True,] . . . it is impossible to form a fixed idea of any of these things as either being what it is or not being what it is, or being both, or being neither . . . .

Well, then, we've discovered that the many things considered beautiful by those who do not recognize the beautiful itself stand between reality and unreality . . . . And we agreed before that if we could find things that are both real [in a sense] and unreal [in a sense], they would be the objects of opinion rather than knowledge [or ignorance] . . . .

I understand and agree.

And what about those who can see the many beautiful things in the world, but who cannot grasp beauty itself and who cannot follow if someone else tries to lead them to knowledge of the beautiful, and who can see many just actions but not justice itself, and so on? What they believe is merely a matter of *opinion*, isn't it, and they do not *know* anything that they believe, isn't that so?

10

That's what we must say.

And those who can see beauty, justice, and so on in themselves, and who grasp the essential and permanent natures of such things, can't we say that they have *knowledge* rather than opinions about such objects?

Absolutely!

Then we will say that these people are lovers of knowledge and wisdom, whereas the others are devotees and lovers of opinion . . . [since they love beautiful things, but do not acknowledge the existence of beauty itself] . . . . Those who seek knowledge of the things themselves we will call *philosophers* (lovers of wisdom) rather than lovers of opinion . . . .

Who should rule the state?

Now, Glaucon, at long last we know the difference between philosophers and non-philosophers . . . . Which of the two, would you say, should rule the state?

I'm not sure.

Well, do you agree that political leaders should be guardians of the laws and customs of the community?

Yes.

And isn't it clear that such a guardian should be a person of vision and not one who is blind?

Of course.

11

But is there any difference between blindness and the mind-set of those we have called non-philosophers? Having no knowledge of what is really real, such people have no model to enlighten their minds. How, then, can they establish or protect the community's standards of right and wrong, good and evil?

I don't see how they can. They are, in a real sense, blind.

So we don't want people like that to be the rulers of the state, do we? Instead, wouldn't it be better for us to appoint as our leaders those who know reality (that is, the philosophers) and who are just as experienced and at least as morally good as the others?

It would be absurd if we didn't . . . .

[So it is agreed, then, that the best society will be ruled by philosophers, that is, those who are wise, good, and competent.]

What good rulers need most to know -- the idea of the Good

[If the rulers of the state are to rule effectively, they must learn the nature of the Absolute Good.] This is the most important thing to know because we can determine what is just or unjust, right or wrong, and so forth, only by comparison with the model of absolute goodness. At this point, though, I feel somewhat at a loss because my own knowledge of the Good is limited. But if we don't find out what the Good is, none of our other knowledge will benefit us. There's no point in having something unless goodness comes with it. Don't you agree?

I certainly do.

12

Now, you must have noticed that most people think that pleasure is the Good, whereas more intelligent people think that the Good is knowledge.

Yes, I have.

And those who think that the good is knowledge are unable to tell us exactly what *kind* of knowledge constitutes goodness, and eventually they are forced to say that it is knowledge of goodness [so that the good is knowledge of the good].

But that's absurd.

Of course it is. People like that blame us for not knowing what the good is, and then they talk to us as if we did know what it is. After all, to say that the good is knowledge of goodness assumes that we know what is meant by "goodness."

You're perfectly right.

What about those who say that the good is pleasure? Aren't they just as lost as the others? Don't they have to admit that there are bad pleasures?

Certainly.

From their point of view, then, it logically follows that the same thing is both good and bad?

So it seems.

Well, then, it's clear that there's plenty of room for disagreement about the nature of the Good .... But it's also clear that no one is satisfied with what is only *apparently* good. Everyone wants

13

what is *really* good . . . . The Good is something that everyone wants; it is the goal of all human activity. And yet, most people have only a vague sense that the Good exists, and they cannot grasp its true nature . . . . But we cannot allow the political leaders of an ideal state, those who are to guide the state and its citizens, to be ignorant of something of this great importance, can we?

No, indeed!

And don't you also agree that anyone who is ignorant of what is good about just and moral conduct will make a pretty poor guardian of the state . . . , whereas one who knows these things will make a proper leader of a well-formed constitution?

Yes, I do . . . . But, Socrates, what do *you* think? Is the Good knowledge, or pleasure, or something else that we have not yet considered?

What a question to ask me! I guess that you will not be content with a review of other people's opinions on these matters!

No, Socrates, for it doesn't seem right for you to be wasting time on other people's views when you yourself have devoted so much of your attention to this issue.

Are you saying that it's OK for someone (like me) to speak as if he knows what he doesn't know?

No, but you should be willing to state your own opinions [even though you have little faith in opinions without knowledge] . . . . We'll be satisfied if you explain the Good in at least a general way . . . .

14

The analogy between the Good and the sun[1]

[Well, I'll give it a try.] But, since I'm really on shaky ground here, I hope you'll allow me to set aside, at least for now, the question as to what the Good itself is . . . . Let's instead focus on something that is a child of the Good and that resembles it closely. OK?

OK . . . .

All right, then, here goes. Didn't we agree earlier that there are many beautiful things, and many good things, and so on, and that we distinguish between them in words?

We did.

And we also spoke of beauty itself, goodness itself, and so on, didn't we? And we said that "the many" of a certain type [for example, beautiful things] all belong to that single type [for example, beauty itself], so that "the many" in a given category share a single essence. Isn't that so?

That's what we said.

And "the many" are visible rather than intelligible, while the essence shared by "the many" is intelligible but not visible?[2]

---

[1]Traditionally called "the simile of the sun."

[2]When Plato distinguishes between the visible (or perceptible) and the intelligible dimensions of reality, he is differentiating between that which can be

15

Yes.

Now, with what sense do we see the things we see?

With the sense of sight.

And we hear audible things with the sense of hearing, and so on with our other senses and other perceptible things?

Yes.

Have you ever considered how generous the creator was when he made the power of seeing and being seen?

What do you mean by that?

Well, look at it this way. Do hearing and sound need another kind of thing for the one to hear and for the other to be heard, some third thing without which there will be no hearing or being heard?

I don't think so.

Nor do most of the other powers of sensation need any such third thing, right?

I can't think of any.

But what about the sense of sight and the power to be seen? They have such a need, don't they?

---

accessed through the senses and those realities that are accessible only through thought or reason.

Again, I don't quite understand what you are getting at.

I mean that someone may have the power of sight and try to use it to see something with certain colors in it, but there will be no seeing and no being seen unless some third thing, which exists for this purpose, is also present.

What are you referring to?

I mean light, of course.

Oh, now I get it.

Then light must be very valuable since it unites the power of sight with the power of being seen, isn't that so?

Yes, indeed.

And which of the gods in heaven is the cause of light? Whose light is it that makes seeing and being seen possible?

The same that you and everyone else would name -- the sun.

And isn't sight naturally related to the sun as follows . . . ? Sight and the sun are not the same; neither the sense of sight itself nor the eye is identical with the sun . . . . And yet, there's no power of sensation that is more like the sun than the power of sight . . . . Furthermore, the ability of the eye to see is received from the overflowing light of the sun. Do you accept these claims?

Yes, I do.

We can conclude, then, that the sun isn't sight itself, but it is the cause of sight and is itself visible. Right?

Right.

This, then, is what I meant earlier when I said that, instead of focusing on the Good itself, we will concentrate on a child of the Good. For there is an analogy between the Good and its offspring, the sun: What the Good is in the intelligible realm, in relation to the mind and to the things known only by the mind, the sun is in the visible realm, in relation to sight and visible things.

I need to hear more about that. I don't grasp it right now.

Well, you know that we can't see things at night as well as we can see them in the daylight. At night, we are almost blind and seem not even to have the potential for seeing clearly . . . . But when we observe things that are illuminated by the sun, then we see quite clearly . . . . Do you follow this?

Of course.

Then can't you see that the mind functions in a similar way? When it is focused on something that stands in the light of truth and reality, then it has understanding and knowledge. But when the mind is directed to things that are unclear (because they are coming into being and then passing out of being [that is, continually changing]), it can form nothing but ever-shifting opinions. The mind then seems devoid of understanding. Isn't that right?

It seems so.

Then it is the Good that gives truth to the things that are known and the power of knowing to the knower. It is the cause of knowledge and truth, and it is also an object of knowledge. But the Good is not identical with knowledge and truth. While they are valuable, the Good is even more so. As in the visible realm, where light and sight are like but not identical with the sun, so in the intelligible realm, knowledge and truth are good, but they are not *the* Good, which is higher than both of them . . . . We can also say that the sun provides visible things, not only with the power of being seen, but also with their coming-into-being, growth, and nourishment (although the sun is not itself the process of coming-into-being); and in the same way, the Good, in addition to giving the power of being known to the objects of knowledge, gives them their very being (although the Good is not being, but rather is superior to it in glory and power) . . . .

[At this point, Socrates seems about to stop his discussion of the Good, but Glaucon begs him to continue.]

The image of the divided line

We've agreed, then, that there are these two things [the Good and the sun], one ruling over the intelligible realm and the other over the visible realm . . . . So there are perceptible things and intelligible things, right?

Yes.

We can represent this by drawing a line (A-E) and then dividing it into two unequal sections (A-C and C-E). [The longer section of the line (C-E) represents the intelligible realm (*to noēton*), which is the object of knowledge (*epistēmē*); and the shorter section (A-C) represents the perceptible realm (*to horāton*), which is the object of opinion (*doxa*).] Then, following the same proportions, we divide each of the two sections of the line accordingly (A-B, B-C, C-D, and D-E). [The length of each of the four sections symbolizes the degree

19

to which that section approaches reality and truth. The line will then appear as follows:[1]]

Perceptible Realm (A-C)   Intelligible Realm (C-E)

A_____B_____C_____D_____E

       Opinion   Knowledge
       (A-C)   (C-E)

The smaller section in the perceptible realm (A-B) represents images of things, by which I mean shadows, reflections . . . , and so forth . . . . The longer section in the perceptible realm (B-C) covers the things whose images, shadows, and reflections are found in the lower section, that is, animals, plants, manufactured things [in fact, all perceptible objects]. Do you see what I'm doing here?

I think so.

Then can we say that, with respect to their relations to reality, the image or shadow of a thing is to the thing itself as the realm of opinion is to the realm of knowledge [that is, closer to reality]?

I can accept that.

[So now the line would be amended as follows (see next page):]

_____

[1]There is no line actually drawn in the Greek text of the *Republic*.

Perceptible Realm (A-C)   Intelligible Realm (C-E)

Images   Perceptible
             Objects

A_____B_____C_____D_____E

      Opinion   Knowledge
       (A-C)   (C-E)

Now, let's divide the section of the line representing the intelligible realm (C-E) as follows: The shorter part of this section (C-D) represents the mind's attempt to achieve knowledge through scientific and mathematical reasoning (*dianoia*), which takes certain "first principles" for granted and then uses things in the perceptible world as images of higher realities that can be known only through reason. This kind of thinking begins with certain unquestioned hypotheses and then reasons out a conclusion. It does not move *to* but *from* first principles. Now, the longer part of this section (D-E) represents the mind's movement from first principles that have been hypothesized to first principles that are completely free from hypotheses. Here, the mind makes no use whatever of images or likenesses, but moves toward truth and reality by way of forms[1] alone, in and of themselves.

That is *really* hard to follow!

Let's discuss it further. Students of geometry and arithmetic and mathematics in general take certain things for granted, for

_____

[1] The highest realities, according to Plato, are "forms" (singular, *eidos*; plural, *eide*). These are non-physical, ideal realities that are accessible, not through the senses, but only through reason.

21

example, that there is a real difference between odd and even numbers, that there are various types of geometrical figures . . . , and so forth. They treat these things as known and as given, and they don't try to prove them to themselves or to anyone else because they think they are perfectly clear to everyone. These assumptions are the starting points of mathematical reasoning, which proceeds from them through a number of steps and arrives at a conclusion.

I understand that.

Then you also understand that, while mathematicians make use of perceptible things in their work, they are interested in such things only in so far as they are likenesses of other [higher] things. For example, they sometimes draw things that *look like* squares and diagonals, but that is only because they are seeking an understanding of *squareness in itself* and of *the diagonal in itself* . . . and of other such things that are, in themselves, imperceptible and that can be grasped only through reason. Are you following this?

Yes.

This is the kind of thinking I meant when I referred to the mind seeking knowledge of the intelligible realm by way of scientific and mathematical [that is, hypothetical] reasoning [represented by section C-D of the divided line] . . . . And the kind of thinking represented on the divided line by the longer section in the intelligible realm (D-E) is *dialectic* (*dialektikē*, that is, philosophical reasoning). Here, hypotheses are not treated as first principles but as stepping stones enabling the mind to reach something that is not hypothetical, namely, the first principle of everything [the Good]. Once reason has grasped this supreme principle, it turns around and, following out the implications of that principle, it deduces its conclusions without the aid of anything perceptible at all. It employs only forms, moving from forms to forms and ending with forms.

22

[Now our line will be filled in further, as below:]

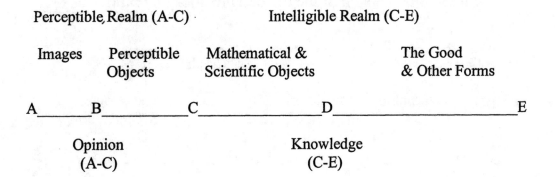

Perceptible Realm (A-C)   Intelligible Realm (C-E)

Images   Perceptible   Mathematical &   The Good
          Objects   Scientific Objects   & Other Forms

A_____B_____C_____D_____E

        Opinion   Knowledge
        (A-C)   (C-E)

I don't grasp everything you're saying [said Glaucon], but I do see that the part of the real and intelligible realm that is the object of those who know how to practice dialectic [philosophical reasoning] is more clear than the part studied by mathematicians and scientists. They take the starting points of their inquiries for granted, and although they approach reality (that is, the intelligible realm) through reasoning rather than through perception, they don't fully understand what they are studying because, proceeding from taken-for-granted hypotheses as they do, their thinking does not go back to a genuine first principle . . . .

I think you've got it. I would only add, on the basis of what we have said, that there are four states of mind corresponding to the objects depicted in the divided line: *philosophical wisdom* (*noēsis*) (knowledge of the forms, especially the Form of the Good); *scientific knowledge* (*epistēmē*) (knowledge of mathematical and scientific objects); *informed opinion* (*pistis*) (based on observation of perceptible things); and *delusion* (*eikasia*) (believing images to be the things they image). Arrange them on the divided line accordingly, assigning to each state of mind a degree of clarity and certainty corresponding to the degree of reality possessed by its objects.

23

I understand and agree, and I will arrange them as you say.

[So the final version of the divided line looks like this:]

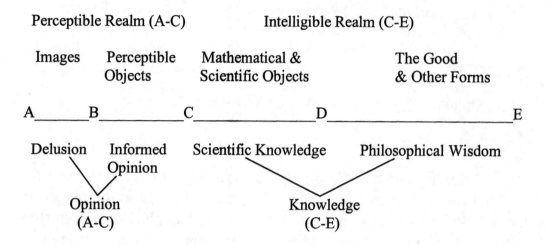

The allegory of the cave

Now [said Socrates], I'm going to describe a fictional situation that illustrates the human situation, that is, with reference to our enlightenment or lack of it. Imagine a group of people imprisoned in a deep cave. At the far end of the cave . . . , there's an opening to the outside world. But the people have been in the cave since they were children, and they have had their legs and necks tied up so as to keep them in one place and to allow them to look only in one direction, that is, straight ahead. At a distance behind them and up a slope in the cave, there's a fire burning, and between the prisoners and the fire there's a road. On the prisoners' side of the road, a wall has been constructed, something like the screen that separates a puppeteer and his puppets from his audience . . . . Imagine also that there are people walking back and forth on the far side of this wall and that they are carrying all kinds of statues of people and of animals (the statues being

24

made of stone, wood, and other materials). While they carry these objects back and forth, some of the people talk, and others remain silent.

This is a strange story [said Glaucon] -- and strange prisoners.

But they're a lot like us, when you think about it. Being bound up as they are, they can't see much of themselves or of one another. For the most part, what they see are the shadows cast by the fire on to the cave wall that they are forced to look at.

That's how it would be if they had to spend their lives unable to move their heads.

And what about the objects being carried back and forth behind them? They'll see only shadows of those things, won't they?

Of course.

Now, what if they could converse with one another? Wouldn't they assume that the words they used applied only to the passing shadows on the wall in front of them?

Absolutely.

And what if sounds from the people behind them were to echo off of the wall they are watching? Wouldn't the prisoners believe that the sounds were coming from the shadows on the wall?

No doubt about it.

For these prisoners, then, reality would be nothing but the shadows on the wall, and they wouldn't be able to recognize any other realities?

That's true.

Then imagine what would happen if they were set free from their imprisonment and liberated from their ignorance. What would that be like? Let's imagine that one of them has been set free and forced to get up, and turn around, and walk about, and look toward the firelight. I'm sure he would find the experience painful and confusing. He wouldn't be able to recognize the objects whose shadows he had previously been looking at, would he? And then suppose that someone tells him that what he had been looking at all his life were illusions and that now he can see more correctly because he is turned in the right direction and is closer to reality. How do you think he'd react to that? And how would he handle it if he were shown the passing objects and asked to identify them? Don't you think he'd be overwhelmed and that he'd believe that the shadows on the wall were more real than the things being shown to him now?

That's for sure!

And if he had to look at the firelight itself, wouldn't this hurt his eyes? And wouldn't he try to run back to the things he can see, thinking that they are really more clear than what is now being shown to him?

He would.

Now, imagine that someone drags him up the rough and steep path leading from the cave to the outside world and forces him out into the daylight. Wouldn't he be pained and distressed by this treatment? Wouldn't the light of the sun blind him so that he wouldn't be able to see a single one of the things outside the cave that we now call real?

No, he wouldn't be able to.

Not, at any rate, until he had become used to his new situation. Gradually, he would be able to discern shadows, and then reflections in water, and eventually he would be able to see the actual things that cast shadows and reflections. Later, at night, he would look up at the heavenly bodies and at the heavens themselves; he'd examine the stars and the moon, but he wouldn't yet be ready to look at the sun and its light during the daytime . . . . But, finally, he *would* see the sun, not merely images of it in water or elsewhere; he'd be able to look at and study the sun itself, in its own proper place. [The diagram on the next page shows the structure of Plato's cave image with parallels to the figure of the divided line.]

That's the way things would go for him.

And at this point, the liberated prisoner would conclude that it is the sun that is the source of the seasons and the yearly cycle. He would come to think that it is the sun that rules over everything in the perceptible world and that it is somehow the cause of everything that he and his fellow prisoners used to see and believe.

That would probably be his next step.

And then, when he thinks of his former situation in the cave and what passed for wisdom there, don't you think that he will be happy with his new situation and feel pity for those still imprisoned?

Definitely.

(continued on p. 29)

Ascent from the Cave
(with Parallels to the Divided Line)

Sun
(Form of the Good)

Dialektikē & Noēsis[1]

Heavens, Stars, Moon
(Lower Forms)

OUTSIDE
WORLD

Objects that Cast Shadows & Reflections
(Scientific & Mathematical Objects)

Dianoia & Epistēmē[2]

Shadows & Reflections
(Physical Representations of Scientific & Mathematical Objects)
↑
———————————] Exit from Cave [———————————
↑

CAVE WORLD

[[[Fire]]]

Pistis[3]

- -
Road
- -

Wall between Prisoners and Road
↑
Upward Slope
↑
Prisoners
x x x x x x x x x

Eikasia[4]

Cave Wall / Shadow Screen

---

[1]Philosophical reasoning and enlightenment.
[2]Scientific and mathematical reasoning and knowledge.
[3]Informed opinion.
[4]Delusion.

28

Now, suppose that, in the cave, the prisoners had the custom of giving honor, praise, and prizes to those who were best at seeing and identifying the passing shadows and remembering which came first, which later, and which at the same time, and who, on this basis, could predict the future. Do you think that our liberated prisoner could take any of this seriously, that he would want any such rewards or would envy anyone who had prestige and power in the cave world? Wouldn't he rather be, in the words of Homer, "a poor slave of a poor master" -- in fact, wouldn't he be willing to put up with just about anything rather than share the opinions and the lives of the prisoners in the cave?

I think that he would rather suffer anything than to live like that.

Let's also consider this. If our man were to go back down into the cave and resume his former place, wouldn't his sudden move out of the sunlight and into the darkness of the cave make him almost blind?

Yes, indeed.

It would, no doubt, take some time for his eyes to become readjusted to the darkness. So what would happen if, before he was accustomed to the darkness again, he had to compete in identifying the shadows with the prisoners who had remained in the cave? Wouldn't he seem ridiculously incompetent? Wouldn't the others say that he had returned from his upward journey with his eyesight ruined and that it isn't good to even try such a trip? And if anyone were to try to free them and take them out of the cave, wouldn't they kill him (if they could get their hands on him)?

They certainly would.

Now, my dear Glaucon, let's apply this allegory to what we were discussing earlier [with reference to the simile of the sun and the image of the divided line]. The perceptible world is like the cave world, and the firelight in the cave is like the power of the sun. The upward journey out of the cave is like the mind's rising from the perceptible realm to the intelligible realm. I hope you can see what I'm getting at, since this is what you wanted to hear about. Whether I'm right about this or not, only God knows, but this is how I see it. In the intelligible realm, the Form of the Good is the last thing to be seen [by the mind], and it is reached only with great difficulty. Once one has seen it, however, one must also see that the Good is the source of all that is true and beautiful in anything, that it creates the sun and its light, and that it is also the source of all truth and knowledge in the intelligible realm. I also think that knowledge of the Good is necessary for anyone to act rationally, whether in private or with reference to public affairs.

I'm following you as best I can.

OK. Then do you see that it's not surprising that those who have made the upward journey don't want to engage in human affairs? What they want is to stay forever in the upper region [in the presence of the Good itself]. But that is to be expected, if our allegory is correct. Right?

Right.

Well, what about this? If someone returns from the divine realm to the human world and its evils, won't he seem clumsy and ridiculous while he's still not seeing well because he has not yet become adjusted to the darkness of the human world? He'll look like a fool if he's forced to argue (in a law court or elsewhere) about the shadows of justice in the human world or about the statues that cast those shadows, especially if he's required to use notions of justice held

30

by people who have no knowledge of justice in itself. Isn't that what's likely to happen?

I wouldn't be surprised.

Here's another point. Common sense tells us that the eyes may be confused in two different ways -- by a change from light to darkness or from darkness to light. Now, the same thing happens to the mind. When we see a person who is troubled and confused, we shouldn't laugh thoughtlessly. Instead, we should try to find out whether his mind has come from a realm of intellectual light into the darkness of this world and, as a result, is temporarily blinded, or whether it is coming from the darkness of ignorance into the light of truth and knowledge and is thus dazzled by the increased brightness. We will then consider the first person happy, and we'll have compassion for the second person. Even if we choose to make fun of the second person [which we shouldn't do], that would be less wrong than if we were to make fun of a mind that has come from the upper light.

That makes a lot of sense [said Glaucon].

Well, if I'm right, then education is not capable of doing what some people think it can do, that is, put knowledge into a mind that doesn't have it, which would be like putting sight into eyes that are blind . . . . What follows from what we've been saying is that the ability to know is present in everyone's mind. If an eye can turn from darkness to light only if the entire body turns, then the mind also must be turned completely away from the ever-changing perceptible realm until it is able to bear the sight of true reality at its most brilliant, that is, until it can behold the Form of the Good. Right?

Right.

31

That's what education should be -- the art of orientation [or re-orientation]. Educators should work out the most effective methods of turning minds around (and these methods should be made as simple as possible). Education should not be an attempt to put sight into a blind eye, so to speak. Instead, it should proceed on the understanding that the mind already has the ability to learn, but that it isn't facing in the right direction or it isn't looking where it ought to look.

I see what you're saying . . . .

Now, think about the uneducated who have no experience of truth as well as those who are now allowed to spend their entire lives in the pursuit of learning. Doesn't it also follow from what we have been saying that neither of these would make good or competent political leaders? The first group [the ignorant] would be no good because they lack direction; they have no single reference point to guide them in all their undertakings, whether public or private. The second group [the learned] would be no good because they have no interest in politics or other practical matters; they imagine that they, while yet living, have already been transported to the Isles of the Blessed.[1]

True.

If, then, we imagine that we are founding a truly good constitution, we must arrange things so that the people with the best natures will pursue that which is most important, namely, the Form of the Good. But once they have ascended to the Good and have had a good look at it, we must not allow them to do what they now do . . . ,

---

[1]In ancient Greek religion, the Isles of the Blessed were the place where the souls of virtuous people would go after death.

32

that is, remain there in the presence of the Good and the other forms, refusing to come back down into the cave world and to the prisoners there. We must make the enlightened come back down and share the work and the rewards of the cave world, regardless of whether such work and rewards are worthless or worthwhile.

But then [exclaimed Glaucon], we'll be harming them, making their lives worse rather than better, won't we?

Remember, my friend, that the aim of the law is not to make any one class in society more happy than the others, but rather to establish the well-being of the community as a whole. The law seeks (whether through persuasion or compulsion) to bring all citizens into harmony with one another and to make each individual share with others whatever good he can contribute to the general welfare. The law should not leave people free to choose their own directions, but should direct people in such a way as to bind the community together.

True, I was forgetting that.

Furthermore, the policy we are discussing would not do any real harm to the philosophers in our community. By forcing them to care for their fellow citizens, we will be treating them justly. We will acknowledge that, in other societies, philosophers arise spontaneously rather than being specifically planned for by the political systems in those societies. It's OK for anything that grows up on its own and doesn't owe its existence to anyone or anything to have no interest in repaying anyone for its upbringing or existence. But in the ideal society that we are thinking about, we must remind our philosophers that their existence is not accidental. They've been planned for and specifically prepared to be rulers of the state . . . , not only for their own good but for that of the entire community. They've received a better and more comprehensive education than philosophers in other societies, and they are more able to play a part in both spheres of life [the intellectual and the practical]. We must tell them that they are obligated to go down to live in the common dwelling place of the community and become used to seeing in the dark. We must say to them, "Once you become used to living in the lower realm, you'll see far, far better than anyone else down there. Because you have seen true beauty, true justice, and true goodness, you will be able to identify every shadow and to recognize what it is a shadow of. But most important, the community (yours as well as ours) will be governed by people who are wide awake, not, as in other societies, by those who quarrel about shadows and struggle against one another for political power, as if that were a highly desirable thing to have. For the truth is that a community is best governed and most free of civil strife when its prospective rulers are least interested in ruling, and it is governed most badly when its rulers are eager to rule." Are you with me, Glaucon?

Yes, I am.

Then do you think that our philosophers will disobey us and refuse to take part in the running of the state (keeping in mind that they can still spend most of their time with one another in the higher realm)?

No, they won't [said Glaucon]. We'll be giving just orders to just people. And they will approach ruling as a burdensome but inescapable duty, which is opposite to the attitudes of people who seek power in other societies.

That's it, Glaucon. We'll have a well-governed community only if we can come up with a way of life for its prospective rulers that is more desirable than ruling! And our philosopher-rulers will be truly rich -- not in gold, but in virtue and rationality. By contrast, in societies run by those who are poor in goodness and reason, and who see a political career as a path to success and happiness for themselves,

34

ruling becomes a thing to be fought for, and this struggle for power destroys the peace of the community.

True.

Other than the philosophical life, can you think of any way of life that disdains political power?

None other.

As a matter of fact, political power should be held by those who do not want it. Otherwise, those who love power will fight against one another for it.

Right.

The best rulers of the state, then, are those who know the Good, who don't look to politics for their happiness, and who live a higher life than the political life. What do you say to that?

Outstanding!

ARISTOTLE
(387-322 BC)

from the

NICOMACHEAN ETHICS[1]

I. The Human Good

The goal-directed nature of human conduct[2]

Human behavior is goal-directed. All distinctively human actions are thought to aim at some good. [A *distinctively human action* is one that is conscious, rational, and voluntary.] *The* good (that is, the "supreme" human good) is a purely final good; it is *the ultimate goal of all human desires and actions*.

We can make a distinction between the goods we pursue. Some things are good because they lead to other things that we desire and consider to be good. So some things can be thought of as *means* to an

---

[1]Translated, paraphrased, and edited by George Cronk. © 1996. The *Nicomachean Ethics* is traditionally divided into ten "books." Books VII, VIII, and IX are not included in this translation. For the Greek text, together with a standard English translation by H. Rackham, see Aristotle, *The Nicomachean Ethics* (Cambridge MA: Harvard University Press, The Loeb Classical Library, 1934).

[2]Book I, Chapter 1. Each of the ten "books" of the *Nicomachean Ethics* is traditionally subdivided into "chapters."

end. It seems clear that, in a means-end relationship, the end is better than the means, that is, the end is the true object of desire, and the means is chosen, not for itself, but because it enables us to reach what we really want.

Now, since there are many actions, arts, and sciences, it would appear that there are many goals pursued by human beings. The goal of medicine is health; shipbuilders seek to build ships; the art of war aims at victory; and the science of property management has wealth as its goal. But, as we have seen, some things are merely means to higher ends. In this sense, we can see that some arts and sciences are higher than others. For example, bridle-making and the other arts concerned with the equipment and training of horses fall under the higher art of horsemanship, and horsemanship and all military activities are secondary to the art of war. So we can make a distinction between major arts and sciences and secondary arts and sciences, for the ends of the secondary arts and sciences are pursued for the sake of the major arts and sciences . . . . [That is, the secondary arts and sciences are pursued as *means* to the ends that are the goals of the major arts and sciences.]

The ultimate human good[1]

We must ask, then, whether there is some end or goal of the things we do that we desire entirely for its own sake (everything else

---

[1]Book I, Chapter 2, 1094^{a}18-25. (The balance of Book I, Chapter 2, and all of Chapter 3, are not included in this translation.) The reference numbers used in this and some later footnotes are to the pages, columns (^{a} = left; ^{b} = right), and lines in Immanuel Bekker's authoritative edition of the Greek text of Aristotle's complete works, published in 1831. This is the standard scholarly convention for exact citations of passages in Aristotle's writings.

being desired because of this) and not at all for the sake of something else. If there is such an ultimate end of human action, then clearly it must be, not just *a* good among others, but rather *the* good, that is, the supreme human good. If there is no such ultimate or final end of human action, then one end is merely a means to some further end, and the latter end is then merely a means to still a further end, and so on to infinity, which would make human desire and action ultimately pointless [since human pursuits would in that case have no final destination to give overall structure, meaning, and direction to our lives].

If human action *does* aim at a single good which is supreme and therefore higher than all other goods, then it would seem very important, if not absolutely essential, to know its nature, so that, like archers with a clear target to aim at, we can orient our lives toward the ultimate good and increase our chances of hitting the mark. So we must try to determine, at least in a general way, what the ultimate human good is . . . .

The nature of the ultimate human good: *eudaimonía*[1]

Since all human knowledge and action aim at some good. . . , just what *is* the highest of all the goods pursued by human activity? There is at least *verbal* agreement on this, for both ordinary and superior people say that it is "happiness" (*eudaimonía*), and they all identify "living well" and "doing well" with being "happy." However, with regard to the exact *nature* or *essence* of happiness, there is much disagreement, and the majority of people [who are not wise] hold

---

[1]Book I, Chapters 4-5. (Book I, Chapter 6, is not included in this translation.)

views on this matter that are quite different from the views held by the wise [who are few in number]. Most people think that happiness is some plain and obvious thing such as pleasure, wealth, or high social status . . . . Among the wise, there are those [such as Plato] who have claimed that, over and above these particular goods, there is another, supreme good, which is good in and of itself and which is the cause of whatever goodness there is in the lesser goals pursued by human beings.

Rather than examining all opinions as to the nature of happiness, which would be rather a waste of time [because it would take so long to do], we shall discuss only those views that are most widespread or that seem to be supported, at least to some extent, by reason and experience . . . .

Judging from the lives they lead, most people, especially those who are the most vulgar, seem . . . to identify happiness with pleasure (*hedoné*). That is why they want nothing better than a life of enjoyment. For there are . . . three major styles of life: (1) the life of enjoyment, (2) the life of political activity, and (3) the life of intellectual inquiry.

The masses of people [seeing pleasure as the purpose of life] evidently have low standards of taste, for they prefer to live like cattle; and there are those in high social or political positions who also live nothing more than lives of sensual indulgence. More refined people with active dispositions [those who live the political life] tend to identify happiness with high social status and political power; but this seems too superficial to be what we are looking for, since social status and political power seem to depend more on those who confer such goods than on those who receive them, while we feel that true happiness is something that belongs to its possessor and that is not easily taken away from him. Furthermore, it seems that people who pursue status and power are trying to convince themselves and others

40

of their own excellence (*areté*) . . . . So it seems that status and power are not actually pursued as ends in themselves, but rather as means to a higher end, namely personal excellence . . . .

So much for the life of enjoyment and the life of social and political advancement. The third type of life, that of intellectual inquiry, we shall examine later on [pp. 66-70, below].

As for the life of money-making [a fourth life-style], it is followed only under some kind of compulsion; and it is clear that wealth is not the good we are seeking to define since it serves only as a means to ends beyond itself . . . .

The general nature of *eudaimonía*[1]

Though apparently there are many goals of human action, we choose some of them (for example, wealth) only as a means to something else. Thus, not all goals are final and complete; but the supreme good is obviously something final and complete. So if there is only one final and complete goal, this will be the good we are looking for; and if there are more than one, the good will be the most final and complete of these.

Now, a goal desired for its own sake is more final and complete than one desired for the sake of something other than itself; and a goal that is pursued for its own sake alone and never for the sake of something else is more final and complete than a goal that is wanted both for its own sake and for the sake of something else. That which is

---

[1]Book I, Chapter 7, 1097^a25-1097^b21.

41

always pursued for its own sake and never for the sake of something else is final and complete without qualification [that is, absolutely].

Happiness, more than anything else, seems to be an absolutely final and complete goal, since it is always desired entirely because of itself and never because of something else beyond it. It is true that we pursue honor, pleasure, understanding, and excellence for their own sakes (since we should be glad to have each of them even though no extraneous benefit resulted from it), but they are also pursued because we believe that they are means to the end of happiness. Happiness, however, is never pursued for the sake of honor, pleasure, etc., nor for the sake of anything other than itself.

The conclusion that happiness is a final and complete end also follows from the generally accepted view that the highest good is sufficient in itself . . . . A good that is sufficient in itself is that which, all by itself, makes life worthwhile and lacking in nothing. We think of happiness as that kind of good.

We also consider happiness to be the most desirable of all things, and we cannot view it as one good among many others. For if happiness were one good among others, then it could be made more desirable by the addition to it of even the smallest of other goods [and the idea of making happiness *more desirable* makes no sense] . . . .

Happiness in general, then, is something final, complete, and sufficient in itself, and, as such, it is the ultimate goal of all human action.

The specific nature of *eudaimonía*[1]

But we are in need of a more specific definition of the nature of happiness. This might be achieved if we could first determine the function (*ergon*) of a human being. The good or "doing well" of anything that has a characteristic function or activity (for example, a flute-player, a sculptor, or any artist) is thought to lie in the performance of that function. The same would appear to be true for a human being as such, if there is a distinctive human function . . . .

What, then, could the distinctive human function be? The mere act of living is shared even by plants [not to mention animals], whereas we are looking for the function that is unique to human nature. We must therefore exclude from our definition the vital activities of nutrition and growth. Next in order would be some sort of sentient life; but sentience is shared by horses, cattle, and animals in general. [It is not distinctively human.] There remains, then, some sort of activity that expresses or actualizes the rational part of human nature (for reason *is* a distinctive property of human nature; it is not possessed by either plants or animals) . . . . Moreover, we are speaking of human rationality, not as a capacity or potentiality, but rather as an activity or actuality.

Now, if the distinctive human function is activity expressive of and in accordance with reason, and if [the difference between] the function of an individual *as such* and the function of a *good* individual of the same class (for example, a harpist and a *good* harpist, and so on generally) is that the former *functions* while the latter functions *excellently* (for example, the function of a harpist is to play the harp, and the function of a *good* harpist is to play the harp well or

---

[1]Book I, Chapter 7, $1097^{b}22$-$1098^{a}18$.

excellently), then . . . it follows that *the human good, which is happiness, is to live in accordance with reason and to do so excellently* . . . . Furthermore, this activity must continue throughout one's lifetime; for one [robin] does not make a spring, nor does one fine day. Similarly, neither can one day or a brief space of time make a human being happy . . . .

External and internal goods[1]

Goods have been divided into three classes: (1) external goods [for example, friends, money, political power]; (2) psychological goods [such as peace of mind]; and (3) bodily goods [such as physical health]. [Psychological goods and bodily goods can be grouped together as *internal* goods because they have their existence *in* the self; that is, they are *perfections* of the self.] Of the three types of goods, we consider psychological goods to be the most valuable, that is, to be good in the fullest sense and to the highest degree . . . .

[On this basis, we can say that happiness (*eudaimonia*) is mainly a psychological (*internal*) good, which expresses itself in excellent *action*. That is, it is a good not just "in possession" but "in use;" it is not just a state of mind, but an *activity* of the self in accordance with excellence; it is, by and large, *living excellently*.]

Furthermore, the active pursuit of excellence, which makes us happy, is also pleasant . . . . Those who live in pursuit of excellence have no need to pursue pleasure as something to be added to excellence; rather, the pursuit of excellence is, in itself, pleasant . . . .

---

[1]Book I, Chapter 8. (Book I, Chapter 9, Chapter 10, 1100^a10-1101^a13, and Chapters 11 and 12 are not included in this translation.)

[The pursuit of pleasure as an end in itself does not lead to excellence, since some pleasures are base and bad; but the pursuit of excellence is, at least in the long run, a pleasant activity and makes for a generally pleasant life.]

While internal goods [both psychological and physical] are essential to a happy and pleasant life, external goods are also necessary to the good life. It is next to impossible to live well without the proper equipment. For example, we need friends, and wealth, and political power in order to pursue happiness effectively . . . . So happiness seems to require external prosperity [or circumstantial security] in addition to the internal psychological and bodily goods spoken of before (and circumstantial security seems to depend to some extent on good fortune) . . . .

Summary statement on the nature of *eudaimonía*

We are now in a position to define the happy person [the "eudaimon"] as one who lives in pursuit of complete human excellence, and who has a sufficient supply of external goods [and thus has circumstantial security], and who lives that way, not for some short period, but throughout a complete lifetime. Happiness (*eudaimonía*), then, is an end that is in every way utterly and absolutely final and complete.[1]

---

[1]Book I, Chapter 10, 1101^{a}14-18.

45

II. Human Excellence and the Good Life

Human nature and the types of human excellence[1]

Since happiness is an active life in pursuit of complete human excellence, we had better examine the nature of such excellence so that we will be able to see more clearly what happiness itself is . . . .

By *human* excellence, we are referring to a psychological good, not to a good of the body. This is consistent with our earlier definition of happiness itself as primarily a psychological activity [or perhaps as the *result* of a certain kind of psychological activity, namely the pursuit of excellence] . . . . [Thus, to discover the nature of human excellence, we must study the structure of the human psyche (Greek, *psuché*), since human excellence *is* the superior functioning of the self.]

The human psyche is partly rational and partly nonrational . . . . [The rational part consists of the intellect, which has the power of *reason*, and reason, as we stated earlier, is the distinctive characteristic of human nature.] Within the nonrational part of the psyche, there are two dimensions. One, which seems common to all living things [plants, animals, and humans], is life, nutrition, and growth. This dimension is essentially *vegetative* in nature . . . , and since this is apparently common to all living things, it is not distinctively human . . . , and thus it reveals no specifically human excellence. [Also, the vegetative dimension of the self is not subject to the rule of reason.]

---

[1]Book I, Chapter 13, 1102^{a}5-1103^{a}3.

46

The other dimension of the nonrational part of the psyche . . . is a power that tends to resist or even combat reason. [This power is *desire*, which gives rise to our appetites and passions.] A person suffering from some sort of bodily paralysis may wish to move his limbs to the right but then find that they swerve to the left, contrary to his intention. Similarly, a person whose passions and appetites are not well-disciplined will not be able to control those impulses that cause him to act contrary to reason . . . . However, our desires *can* be controlled by reason, since there *are* people (for example, those who are self-disciplined and morally strong) whose desires and actions seem to be in harmony with and obedient to reason . . . and since we can sometimes persuade others to act rationally through the use of warnings, reprimands, and encouragements . . . .

Intellectual and moral excellence[1]

Based upon the distinction between the intellectual and desiring elements in human nature, we therefore distinguish between two main types of human excellence: *intellectual excellence* (which refers to excellent thinking and reasoning) and *moral excellence* (which refers to excellence of character or to *desiring and acting in accordance with reason*) . . . . Intellectual excellence is acquired through instruction, study, and learning, and thus takes time and requires much experience. [But how is moral excellence acquired?]

---

[1]Book I, Chapter 13, $1103^a4\text{-}10$, and Book II, Chapter 1, $1103^a14\text{-}16$.

47

III. Moral Virtue

How do we become morally excellent?[1]

We become morally excellent (or virtuous) by forming good habits . . . . It is therefore obvious that none of the various types of moral excellence arise in us by nature, since nothing that is what it is by nature can be altered by habituation. For example, it is the nature of a stone to move downwards [toward the center of the earth], and it cannot be trained to move upwards, even if you repeatedly throw it up into the air . . . . However, while we do not become morally excellent by nature, becoming morally excellent is not contrary to nature either. The truth is that nature gives us a potentiality for moral goodness, and this potentiality is actualized by way of habit-formation . . . .

To actualize our potential for moral excellence, we must perform and practice morally good actions . . . . We become just by performing just actions, temperate by performing temperate actions, courageous by acting courageously. We can see this in the political process, since legislators try to make citizens good by way of laws that are intended to train people in the performance of right actions. This is the goal of all legislation, and if the law does not reach this goal, then it is a failure. This is what makes a good constitution different from a bad one . . . .

So moral excellence is a product of good and effective moral training. Thus, it makes no small difference whether we form habits of one kind or another in our youth. It makes a very great difference. In

---

[1]Book II, Chapter 1, 1103^a16-1103^b25.

48

fact, it might make *all* the difference in our becoming virtuous people rather than bad people.

What is moral excellence?[1]

We must now consider what moral excellence is . . . . In general, it is a disposition or state of character [acquired through habituation] that leads a person to function well. [More specifically, moral excellence is the disposition to choose and act in accordance with reason with respect to what we desire.][2]

What does this mean? Well, we can see that moral virtue is destroyed by deficiency and by excess . . . . Just as both excessive and too little exercise undermine one's physical strength, and eating and drinking too much or too little destroy one's physical health (whereas the right quantities of exercise, food, and drink produce, increase, and preserve our strength and health), so it is with temperance, courage, and the other moral virtues. One who fears and runs from everything . . . becomes a coward, and one who fears nothing but rather rushes to meet every danger becomes reckless; and one who indulges in every pleasure and abstains from none becomes degenerate, while a person who rejects all pleasures becomes dead to the world. Courage and temperance, then, are obviously destroyed by excess and deficiency, while they are cultivated and preserved by the avoidance of too much and too little, that is, by the pursuit of the *mean*

---

[1]Aristotle's discussion of the general nature of moral virtue is contained in Book II, Chapters 1-6 and 8-9. Chapters 3-5 and 8-9 are not included in this translation.

[2]Traditional location, Book II, Chapter 5, 1105^b19, and Book II, Chapter 6, $1106^a22\text{-}23$.

49

[that which is intermediate between the extremes of excess and deficiency] .... [1]

Now,[2] the mean sought by moral virtue is not an objective, mathematical mean, but rather a mean that is relative to the individual. An objective mean, which is one and the same for all people, is a mean that is equidistant from each of the extremes. For example, on a scale of numbers from 2 to 10, 6 is the mean between them, as the following diagram shows:

$$2......3......4......5......6......7......8......9......10$$
$$\wedge$$

But the mean that is the goal of moral action is not the same for everybody. Suppose that ten pounds of food is too much for an athlete and that two pounds is too little. It does not follow that an athletic trainer will prescribe six pounds for his trainees. Six pounds might be too much for one athlete and too little for another .... So while the morally virtuous person seeks to avoid moral excesses and deficiencies, he is trying to find, not an objective mean, but rather a mean relative to the individual and to the circumstances in which the individual is situated [that is, a relative mean] ....

Now, moral virtue aims at the mean with regard to both passions (feelings, emotions) and actions. Instead of having too much or too little fear, confidence, desire, anger, pity, etc., and instead of

---

[1]Traditional location, Book II, Chapter 2, $1104^{a}11$-26. (The balance of Book II, Chapter 2, is not included in this translation.)

[2]The rest of this section is a translation of Book II, Chapter 6, $1106^{a}24$-$1106^{b}35$.

50

pursuing pleasure or avoiding pain too much or too little, a person of excellent character (moral virtue) will have the right passions at the right times, with reference to the right objects, towards the right people, for the right purpose, and in the right way, and he will choose and act accordingly . . . . Given this definition of moral virtue, it would appear that it is easy to miss the mark and difficult to hit it [that is, it seems that vice will be more common than virtue].

Summary statement on the nature of moral excellence

To summarize, we may say that moral virtue is a settled disposition of the self that leads to the choice of the mean (that is, the mean relative to the individual and his situation), this being determined by reason or practical wisdom. It is a mean between two vices, that which is excessive and that which is deficient, for the vices fall short of or exceed what is right in both passions and actions, while virtue both finds and chooses that which is intermediate [the mean] . . . .[1]

A limitation on the doctrine of the mean[2]

However, the doctrine of the mean does not apply to every action and to every passion. There are feelings (such as malice, shamelessness, and envy) and actions (for example, adultery, theft, and murder) that are bad in themselves. It is impossible to ever be right with regard to such feelings and actions; they are always wrong. It is absurd to speak of committing adultery with the right woman, at the right time, in the right way; and it is also absurd to think that one can find the mean between excess and deficiency in unjust, cowardly, or

[1]Book II, Chapter 6, 1106^b35-1107^a5.

[2]Book II, Chapter 6, 1107^a9-25.

51

depraved actions. At that rate, there would be a mean [or reasonable amount] of excess and of deficiency, an excess of excess, and a deficiency of deficiency . . . .

The doctrine of the mean is simply not relevant to passions or actions that are either absolutely evil (like the examples mentioned above) or absolutely good (for example, the virtues of temperance and courage and the actions that flow from them). A passion or action that is absolutely evil or absolutely good has no mean, nor does it have any excess or deficiency . . . . In general, there is no mean (or "right amount") of either excess or deficiency, nor is it possible for passions and actions that are in accordance with the mean (that is, "right" passions and actions) to be wrong (that is, excessive or deficient).

Specific moral virtues

So far, we have been discussing moral excellence in general. But there are many specific moral virtues, and we should look at some of these . . . . [1] [The chart on the next page (entitled "Table of Virtues and Vices")[2] summarizes our analysis of a number of virtues and vices.] The chart does not contain anything about justice . . . , which we will discuss later [pp. 55-58, below]; and similarly we will also discuss the various kinds of intellectual excellence later on [pp. 63-66, below] . . . .

---

[1]See traditional editions, Book II, Chapter 7; Book III, Chapters 6-12; Book IV; and Book V (on Justice).

[2]Derived from Book II, Chapter 7, 1107^a28-1108^b10. Aristotle's discussion here is evidently based on a chart or diagram such as this.

52

TABLE OF VIRTUES AND VICES

Sphere of Action or Feeling	Excess (Vice)	Mean (Virtue)	Deficiency (Vice)
fear and confidence	recklessness	courage	cowardice
pursuit of pleasure and avoidance of pain	mindless hedonism (intemperance)	temperance	not enjoying life's pleasures
getting and spending money (minor)	being a spendthrift* (wastefulness)	generosity	stinginess**
getting and spending money (major)	extravagance* (ostentation)	lavish generosity	miserliness** (being really cheap in a big way)
pursuit of great honor and prestige	vanity	self-esteem	low self-esteem
pursuit of small-scale honor and prestige	aggressive ambition	proper ambition	lack of ambition
anger	rage	even-temperedness	lack of spirit (being a wimp)
self-expression	boastfulness (being a braggart)	truthfulness	false modesty or self-deprecation
humor	clownishness	wittiness	humorlessness (no sense of humor)
sociability	self-serving flattery	friendliness (amiability)	cantankerousness (grouchiness, surliness)
sense of shame	being ashamed of everything	modesty	shamelessness
with regard to the good fortune of others	envy	pleasure when good fortune is deserved; pain (righteous indignation) when good fortune is undeserved	malice and spite (enjoyment of the undeserved good fortune and mis-fortune of others)

*Concentrates too much on spending and not enough on getting and saving.

**Concentrates too much on getting and keeping and too little on spending.

53

The major moral virtues: courage, temperance, and justice

[Of all the moral virtues, courage, temperance, and justice are the most important.] **Courage** (*andreia*),[1] as we have seen, is a mean in relation to feelings of fear and confidence . . . . [It is a mean between recklessness and cowardice with regard to that which is fearful.] One who faces up to that which is truly fearful for the right reasons and in the right way and at the right time is courageous . . . .

Furthermore, people are called courageous for enduring pain . . . , and the courageous endurance of pain is rightly praised, for it is harder to bear pain than it is to abstain from pleasure. [But the endurance of pain is often necessary to the achievement of the good. In fact, courage is, to a large extent, the willingness and ability to endure pain when necessary to the achievement of some real and substantial good.]

Temperance (*sophrosuné*)[2] is a mean with regard to the pursuit of pleasure . . . . A person who is excessive with regard to pleasure pursues all pleasures and avoids all pains . . . ; and at the other extreme is the (rare) person who is utterly incapable of enjoying the pleasures of life. Steering a middle course between these two extremes, which are vices, the temperate person pursues and enjoys good pleasures in a moderate way; he avoids all wrong pleasures; and he is not distressed by the absence of pleasure . . . . [Using a definition that is structurally similar to that of our earlier definition of courage, we can say that temperance is the willingness and ability to forego pleasure when

---

[1]Traditional location, Book II, Chapter 7, $1107^a35\text{-}1107^b4$; and Book III, Chapters 6-9.

[2]Traditional location, Book II, Chapter 7, $1107^b4\text{-}8$; and Book III, Chapters 10-12.

54

necessary to the achievement of some real and substantial good.] The temperate person, following the dictates of reason, desires the right things in the right way and at the right time . . . .

[In Book VII, Chapters 1-10, not included in this translation, Aristotle discusses several other character states concerned with the pursuit of pleasure and the avoidance of pain. Two of these are moral strength (continence, *enkrateia*) and moral weakness (incontinence, *akrasía*). These two character states are similar to but not identical with temperance and mindless hedonism (intemperance), respectively. A morally strong (continent) person, like a temperate person, follows reason by neither pursuing pleasure nor avoiding pain excessively, but, unlike a temperate person, he *desires* an excess of pleasure and a deficiency of pain. A morally strong person recognizes that he has bad desires but, through rational self-control, does not follow them. A morally weak (incontinent) person pursues pleasure and avoids pain excessively under the influence of unruly passions, but he knows that his actions are wrong and therefore regrets them, whereas an intemperate person, also motivated by bad desires, acts excessively with regard to pleasure and pain, but thinks (incorrectly) that he is doing the right thing and thus has no remorse concerning his excesses.]

Justice (*dikaiosunê*)[1] is a state of character that inclines one to perform just acts, and to behave in a just way, and to wish for what is just; and injustice (*adikia*) is a character state inclining a person to act unjustly and to wish for unjust things . . . . [More specifically,] the

---

[1] Aristotle's theory of justice is elaborate and complicated. This translation contains only a small part of his overall discussion and analysis of the concept of justice. His full treatment of the subject is contained in the ***Nicomachean Ethics***, Book V, and in Book X, Chapter 9 (1179^b20-1181^b12), and in the ***Politics***, Book III.

word "unjust" (*adikos*) is used to describe one who breaks the law as well as one who takes unfair advantage of another. Evidently, then, the law-abiding and fair person is "just" (*dikaios*). Therefore, it seems that justice is lawfulness and fairness, while injustice refers to that which is unlawful and/or unfair . . . . (Justice [in general] is the only virtue that specifically aims at the good of others . . . .)[1]

Being unfair to another is, with regard to that which is good, taking more than one's fair share and thus depriving the other of his fair share; with regard to that which is bad, unfairness is taking *less* than one's fair share, which means that the other will get *more* than his fair share of evil. [So to be fair and therefore just in our interactions with others we must share both goods and evils with them in an equitable way.]

In addition to fairness, we have also said that to be just is to abide by the law. This implies or presupposes that the laws created by the state through its legislative authority are in some sense just -- that is, in the sense that the laws are aimed at the common good of society, which is the production or preservation of the happiness of the political community. [In seeking to produce and preserve the happiness of the community,] the laws . . . command us to act in a morally virtuous way [that is, to exercise *all* of the moral virtues (courage, temperance, etc.)], and they forbid us to act contrary to moral virtue (that is, wrongly or viciously). The law commands us rightly if it has been rightly enacted;

---

[1]Traditional location of sentence in parentheses, Book V, Chapter 1, 1130^a3-4.

but the commands of the law may not be right if the law has been badly framed.[1]

Therefore, justice in the sense of lawfulness [and on the assumption that the laws of the state are themselves good] is *complete* moral virtue because it requires us to live a completely virtuous life directed, not only at our own happiness, but also at the well-being of others . . . . Justice in this sense ["universal justice"] is not just one moral virtue among the others already discussed. Rather, it is the *whole* of moral virtue . . . . When we exercise moral virtue for the sake of our own happiness, we are "merely" virtuous; but when we act virtuously toward others for the sake of their well-being, we are *just* (in the sense of universal justice) . . . .

[Being fair in our interactions with others is only *part* of complete moral virtue.] It is clear, then, that besides universal justice [which is the whole of moral virtue] there is another kind that we can call "particular" or "partial" justice . . . , which is distinguishable from moral virtue as a whole . . . .

To be just in the "particular" sense, we must give and take in accordance with two basic principles: the *principle of equality* and the *principle of assignment by desert (or merit)*. That is, persons who are

---

[1]This last remark suggests that, in defining one kind of justice as lawfulness, Aristotle is thinking of truly just laws. In the *Politics*, he distinguishes between good and bad governments. One difference between these is that good governments make good laws (that is, laws encouraging moral virtue and serving the common good), while bad governments make bad (unjust) laws. So here, in the *Nicomachean Ethics*, where he describes the law-abiding person as just, Aristotle must be assuming that the laws in question are just laws established by a good government. Otherwise, what he says here would be false, or at least highly debatable.

57

equally deserving must receive equal shares, and persons who are not equally deserving should receive unequal shares. No one should get either more or less than what he deserves. Under the principles of "particular justice," it is unjust when persons who are equally deserving possess or are given unequal shares, or when persons who are not equally deserving possess or are given equal shares . . . . [So when goods (such as honor, wealth, and opportunities) are distributed, no one should get too much or too little, and who gets what should be determined on the basis of individual merit. When penalties and punishments are imposed, they should be imposed only on those who deserve them and, of those who are penalized or punished, no one should be penalized or punished too much or too little.]

[Both universal justice and particular justice observe the principle of the mean. Universal justice is a mean because it is the exercise of all the moral virtues, which are themselves means; and particular justice is a mean because it is equity and fairness, which stand between "too much" and "too little" in the sphere of giving and taking both goods and evils.]

IV. Deliberation and Choice: The Preconditions of Moral Responsibility[1]

We have seen that moral excellence is concerned with feelings and actions. Now, feelings and actions that are voluntary are either praised or blamed, whereas those that are involuntary are often pardoned and sometimes even pitied. Thus, we must try to define the differences between the voluntary and the involuntary . . . .

---

[1]Traditional location, Book III, Chapters 1-5.

Involuntary action

There are two types of involuntary actions: (1) those performed under compulsion and (2) those done on the basis of ignorance. An act is performed under compulsion when it is caused by a force external to the agent and when the agent contributes nothing to it, for example, when a person is carried somewhere by the wind or by people who have him in their power.

But what about actions done out of fear of something worse or for the sake of some higher good (for example, where a tyrant having a man's parents or children in his power orders the man to do something dishonorable as a condition of saving the lives of his family members, or where a ship captain causes his cargo to be thrown overboard during a storm in order to save his ship)? Are these actions voluntary or involuntary? They appear to be "mixed," that is, partly voluntary and partly involuntary. Nonetheless, they are more voluntary than involuntary because, when they are performed, they are matters of choice . . . and it is [at least to some extent] in the agent's power to act or not . . . . [Such acts, therefore, are not completely compulsory. The agent may be motivated to act by an external force, but he contributes to the act through his choice.]

[As stated above, the second kind of involuntary action is action performed on the basis of ignorance.] A person acts on the basis of ignorance[1] when he lacks knowledge of the particular circumstances of

---

[1]In his full discussion of acts based on ignorance, Aristotle distinguishes (1) between acts done *in* ignorance and those done *through* ignorance and (2) between acts based on ignorance which are *in*voluntary as opposed to those that are *non*voluntary. See Book III, Chapter 1, $1110^b18\text{-}32$. These fine distinctions have been excluded from the present translation.

59

his action . . . . It is on these circumstances of action that pity and forgiveness depend because a person who is ignorant of any of these is acting involuntarily . . . . These particular circumstances of action are: (1) the agent; (2) the act; (3) the object of the act (that is, the thing or person being acted on) . . . ; (4) the instrument being used (for example, a tool of some sort); (5) the aim or purpose of the act; and (6) the manner in which the act is being done (for example, gently or violently) . . . .

Now, no one in his right mind could be ignorant of *all* of the particular circumstances of his action. He could not be ignorant of (1) the identity of the agent (that is, himself), but (2) he might not realize what he is doing . . . , or (3) he might mistakenly think . . . that his son was an enemy [and treat him as such], or (4) that a spear had a safety tip on it when it didn't, or that a stone was a piece of pumice [and therefore not a lethal instrument], or (5) one might kill someone with medicine intended to save the person's life, or (6) strike one's opponent in a wrestling match when one only meant to grab the opponent's hand . . . . An agent who is ignorant of any of these circumstances or aspects of action is acting involuntarily . . . .

Voluntary action

If an involuntary act is one performed either under compulsion or on the basis of ignorance, then a voluntary act would appear to be one caused by the agent himself in a situation where he knows (is not ignorant of) the particular circumstances of his action . . . .

Some, but not all, voluntary actions are products of *choice*. For example, the acts of children and animals may be voluntary, but they are not the results of choice [because children and animals are incapable of choice since they cannot reason]; and actions on the spur of the moment, which are done without thinking, are also voluntary but not chosen . . . . What, then, is choice? Since choosing seems to require

60

thinking and reasoning, it must be the result of prior deliberation (forethought, premeditation) . . . .

Now, unless we are stupid or insane, we do not deliberate about things over which we have no control (for example, the order of the universe) or about things that cannot be done [for example, drawing a round square] . . . . We deliberate only about those things that are up to us and that can be done by us . . . . Furthermore, we do not deliberate about ends but only about means to the ends we seek. For example, doctors don't deliberate about *whether* to cure their patients, nor do orators deliberate about *whether* to persuade an audience, nor do good political leaders deliberate about *whether* to produce law and order, nor does anyone else deliberate about the end at which he is aiming. What people deliberate about is *how* they can best reach the goals they set for themselves . . . .

Choice, then, is decision based on deliberation, which is a process of thinking about how we should act in order to reach our goals. [So some voluntary actions are actions resulting from choice, which is itself a product of deliberation.]

Moral freedom and personal responsibility

Now, we desire to reach our goals because we believe them to be good . . . . [1] But the means to a goal or end is the focus of deliberation and choice, and the actions that are necessary to the means are performed in accordance with choice and are therefore voluntary . . . . This shows that the choice between virtue and vice is up to us, for where we are free to act, we are also free not to act; and where we are

---

[1]See Book III, Chapter 4, which is not included in this translation, on the difference between real and apparent goods.

61

free to refuse, we are also free to comply. So if we are free to do a thing when it is right, we are also free not to do it when it is wrong; and if we are free not to do it when it is right, we are also free to do it when it is wrong. But if it is up to us to do or not to do either right or wrong, and if doing right or wrong is what makes us good or bad, then it follows that it is in our power to be virtuous or vicious . . . .

If we are the originators of our own actions . . . , and if we cannot place the responsibility for our actions on anyone or anything other than ourselves, then those actions are in our power, that is, voluntary [and we are responsible for them] . . . . This view is supported by the fact that both private individuals and the laws of society impose blame and punishments upon wrongdoers (except where the offense is committed under compulsion or on the basis of ignorance for which the agent himself is not responsible) and bestow praise and rewards on those who act virtuously. Now, praising, blaming, rewarding, and punishing seem to be aimed at encouraging virtuous behavior and discouraging wrongdoing. But it makes no sense to encourage a person to do an act that he is not free to do or to discourage a person from doing an act that he can't help doing (for example, there is no point in our requiring or forbidding people to feel heat or pain or hunger or the like since they will or will not feel them no matter what we say). [So praising, blaming, rewarding, and punishing imply the reality of moral freedom and personal responsibility.]

The laws even punish wrongful acts based on ignorance in cases where the offender is considered to be responsible for his ignorance. For example, there are severe penalties for wrongs done in a state of drunkenness since the source of the action is in the agent himself; his drunkenness is the cause of his ignorance, but he was capable of not getting drunk. Also, ignorance of the law is no excuse in cases where the agent ought to know what the law is and where it is not difficult to find that out. Indeed, whenever a person violates the law on the basis of ignorance, he is held responsible if his ignorance is due to his own negligence. This is on the assumption that it was in his power not to be ignorant . . . .

V. Intellectual Excellence[1]

[Earlier (pp. 46-47, above),] we distinguished between excellence of character (moral virtue) and excellence of intellect (intellectual virtue). Now that we have discussed moral excellence and the particular moral virtues, let's spend some time on intellectual excellence and the particular intellectual virtues.

We have seen that there are two parts of the human psyche, one rational and one nonrational. We must now make a similar distinction with regard to the rational part of the psyche (the intellect) [since intellectual excellence in general is excellent reasoning] . . . . On the one hand, we study and think about things that cannot be other than they are [the realm of necessity]; and on the other hand, we study and think about things that can be other than they are [the realm of contingency] . . . . Let us call the first theoretical reasoning (*epistemonikon*) and the second practical or deliberative reasoning (*logiotikon*) . . . . Now, the attainment of truth is the aim of both aspects of the intellect;[2] so the excellence of each will be that tendency that enables it to reach the truth . . . .

---

[1]Aristotle's full discussion of intellectual excellence in general and of the particular intellectual virtues is contained in Book VI of the *Nicomachean Ethics*. Only a small portion of Book VI is included here.

[2]Theoretical reasoning aims at truth as an end in itself; and practical reasoning aims at truth that is useful for practical purposes.

There are five ways by which the intellect arrives at truth . . . [that is, there are five particular intellectual virtues]: (1) artistry and craftsmanship (*techné*); (2) inferential knowledge (*epistēmē*); (3) practical wisdom (*phronesis*); (4) theoretical wisdom (*sophia*); and (5) intuitive knowledge (*nous*[1]) . . . . [(1) artistry and craftsmanship and (3) practical wisdom are virtues of the part of the intellect that engages in practical-deliberative reasoning; and (2) inferential knowledge, (4) theoretical wisdom, and (5) intuitive knowledge are virtues of the part of the intellect that engages in theoretical reasoning.]

Excellence in practical reasoning

In the realm of practical-deliberative reasoning (which seeks truth as to things that can be other than they are), we can distinguish between the activities of making and doing . . . . [2]

Artistry and craftsmanship is the activity of making, building, or producing [useful and/or beautiful things] in accordance with a correct process of reasoning. The lack of artistry and craftsmanship results from incorrect reasoning in the process of making, building, or production . . . . [3]

Practical wisdom is knowledge of what is good for human beings (both for particular individuals and for humanity in general) and the ability to deliberate, choose, and act in accordance with such

---

[1]*Nous* ordinarily means "intellect" or "reason," but at this point Aristotle uses the word to describe the intuitive grasping of evident and self-evident truths, that is, truths not arrived at by inference but by direct mental apprehension.

[2]Traditional location, Book VI, Chapter 4, 1140ᵃ1.

[3]Traditional location, Book VI, Chapter 4, 1140ᵃ6-23.

knowledge . . . . It is, therefore, a form of reasoning that grasps the truth concerning action in relation to what is good [and bad] for human beings . . . . [1]

Excellence in theoretical reasoning

[Theoretical reasoning, as stated above, is concerned with things that cannot be other than they are -- that is, things that are necessary, eternal, and universal rather than contingent, temporal, and particular.] *Inferential knowledge* . . . is the apprehension of necessary and eternal truths that are validly deduced from principles that are established through induction . . . . [2] [The conclusion of a valid deductive argument is *necessarily* true (that is, it must be true and cannot be false) *if* the premises of the argument are true.]

There are therefore principles or premises from which deductive reasoning proceeds, but which are not themselves arrived at by deduction. Rather, these "first principles" are established inductively . . . . More specifically, these first principles are grasped directly (that is, not inferentially) by the mental power of *intuition* [which is the comprehension of the evident and self-evident truths that constitute the foundations of deductive reasoning] . . . . [3]

Theoretical wisdom (the highest intellectual virtue) is a combination of intuitive and inferential knowledge (*nous* and *epistēmē'*). The wise person knows (by inference) what follows from

---

[1]Traditional location, Book VI, Chapter 5, 1140^{a}24-30.

[2]Traditional location, Book VI, Chapter 3, 1139^{b}19-36.

[3]Traditional location, Book VI, Chapter 6, 1140^{b}31-1141^{a}8.

65

the first principles, and he also comprehends (through intuition) the first principles themselves . . . . [1]

VI. The Good Life: Concluding Discussion[2]

The highest happiness[3]

If happiness (*eudaimonía*) is acting in a personally excellent way, it seems reasonable to say that it is acting in accordance with the highest form of human excellence (*areté*), and this will be the excellence of the best part of human nature. This is the intellect or whatever else rules and leads human nature toward the noble and the divine . . . . It is the excellent functioning of this part that will constitute perfect happiness.

Therefore, it seems that the best life is the life of intellectual inquiry and theoretical thought, since the intellect is the best part of human nature and since the objects of intellectual inquiry and theoretical thought are the highest things that can be known. Intellectual inquiry is also the most continuous activity, for we can carry it on more continuously than we can any other activity. Furthermore, we have said that happiness must contain an element of pleasure.[4]

---

[1]Traditional location, Book VI, Chapter 7, 1141ᵃ9-19.

[2]See Book X, Chapters 1-9. Only Chapters 7 and 8 are included in this translation.

[3]Book X, Chapter 7.

[4]Aristotle discusses pleasure in two sections of the *Nicomachean Ethics*: Book VII, Chapters 11-14, and Book X, Chapters 1-5. These sections are not

Now, intellectual inquiry is the most pleasant of all excellent endeavors, and philosophy in particular (that is, the pursuit of wisdom) contains pleasures of marvelous purity and permanence. Also, it is fair to say that those who possess knowledge live more pleasantly than those who are still pursuing it.

Intellectual inquiry is also the most self-sufficient activity. Like anyone else, of course, the wise person (*sophos*) requires the [external] necessities of life [bodily health, food, shelter, clothing, etc.]; but so long as these have been adequately supplied . . . , he can engage in theoretical investigations all by himself, and the more he does so the wiser he becomes. It may be that he will make more progress with the help of colleagues, but still he is the most self-sufficient of people.

Another point here is that intellectual inquiry is the only activity that is loved entirely for its own sake. Theoretical thought produces no results beyond itself, whereas we expect practical activities to result in practical benefits beyond themselves.

Finally, the intellectual life appears to be the most leisurely life [as compared with the lives of those who engage in the practice of business, warfare, and politics]. The latter activities allow for little or no leisure, and they are not chosen for their own sakes but rather in order to attain some good beyond themselves (for example, business is carried on in order to make leisure possible, war is waged in order to

---

included in this translation. Aristotle denies that pleasure is the supreme good, but he also denies that pleasure is always bad. His view is that pleasure, while it is not *the* good, is *a* good and that the good life is generally pleasant. Human beings naturally pursue pleasure and avoid pain. Sometimes this is consistent with living a good life, and sometimes it is not. Practical wisdom must decide the issue. The pursuit of pleasure is not always good, but the pursuit of the good brings us pleasure.

establish peace, and those who participate in politics do so in order to attain positions of authority and honor, or to make happiness possible both for the politician and for the community) . . . .

[For these reasons, then, it is the life of intellectual inquiry and theoretical thought] that constitutes complete human happiness . . . . In fact, we can add to what we have said the view that the intellectual life takes a person beyond a merely human level of existence . . . , for the intellect is the *divine* element in human nature . . . and may be said to be the *true self* of the human individual since it is the dominant feature of human nature . . . .

Human happiness and the gods

It is generally believed that the gods enjoy supreme felicity and perfect happiness . . . . We think of the gods as living and acting, not as being always asleep like Endymion[1] . . . . And since it makes no sense to think of the gods as striving to be morally virtuous (since they are already morally perfect), it would appear that their characteristic activity is the contemplation of being and truth [an activity analogous to or identical with the life of theoretical thinking followed by some humans]. Therefore, among human activities, that which is most like the divine activity of contemplation will be the greatest source of happiness. [This human activity is intellectual inquiry, and this is the activity by which humans can become like the gods.][2]

---

[1] In Greek mythology, Endymion was loved by the moon-goddess, who made him immortal, but at the price of permanent unconsciousness.

[2] Traditional location, Book X, Chapter 8, 1178^{b}9-24.

68

It also seems likely that those who pursue the intellectual life . . . are also most loved by the gods. For if, as is commonly believed, the gods oversee human affairs, then it is reasonable to assume that they are pleased with that part of human nature which is best and most akin to themselves, that is, the intellect, and that they bless those who value and honor this most . . . . Therefore, the lover of wisdom is most loved by the gods and consequently most happy . . . . [1]

The second best life

The life of moral virtue also produces happiness for its practitioners. However, in comparison with the intellectual life, the life of moral action is happy only to a secondary degree. The pursuit of moral excellence (as stated above) is not a divine activity, but is rather purely human. [Some of our reasons for saying this are that] being morally virtuous has a lot to do with the rational control of the body and of the passions [and the body and the passions are not the highest elements in human nature], and it is practical-deliberative reasoning [that is, not the higher, divine activity of theoretical reasoning] that guides us in the direction of moral virtue . . . . [2]

Summary statement

What we stated earlier applies here again: that which is best and most pleasant for any creature is that which is proper to its nature. Thus, the life of the intellect is the best and most pleasant life for a human being, inasmuch as the intellect is *the* distinctive component of

---

[1]Traditional location, Book X, Chapter 8, 1179^a23-32.

[2]Traditional location, Book X, Chapter 8, 1178^a9-22.

human nature. The intellectual life, therefore, is the happiest human life.[1]

---

[1]Traditional location, Book X, Chapter 7, 1178^a5-8.

ANSELM OF CANTERBURY
(1033-1109 AD)

from the

PROSLOGION[1]

The Ontological Argument for the Existence of God

[Recently,] . . . I began to ask myself whether it would be possible to construct an argument that would require no support other than itself alone and that would, all by itself, prove that God truly exists . . . . So I seriously devoted my attention to this matter. Sometimes I thought that I was about to grasp what I was looking for, and then it would escape me completely. Then I gave up hope. I decided to stop chasing after something that could not be found. But when I tried to put the idea out of my mind (since I did not want to allow useless speculation to prevent me from concentrating on things I could actually do), it began to haunt me more and more, even though I

---

[1]Translated, paraphrased, and edited by George Cronk. © 1996. "Proslogion" (Greek) and "Proslogium" (Latin) mean "discourse" or "speech directed to another." The *Proslogion* was composed in Latin. It is a short theological and philosophical manual containing a preface and twenty-six chapters. See *St. Anselm's Proslogion*, including the Latin text and a standard translation, with an introduction and philosophical commentary, by M.J. Charlesworth (Notre Dame: University of Notre Dame Press, 1979). The present translation contains portions of the preface and the first chapter and all of chapters 2, 3, and 4.

made a concerted effort to resist it. And then, one day, when I was exhausted as a result of this mental struggle, the proof I had given up on suddenly emerged from the turmoil of my thoughts, so that I then enthusiastically embraced the very idea that I had been trying so hard to cast out of my mind . . . . [1]

Faith seeking understanding[2]

[Oh, Lord my God,] I am not trying to fully understand your nature -- my mind is in no way capable of that! But I do long to gain some understanding of your truth, which I believe and love in my heart. I do not seek understanding as a prelude to faith; on the contrary, *I believe in order to understand* [*Credo ut intelligam*]. For I, like St. Augustine, am convinced that "unless I believe, I shall not understand."

The nature and existence of God[3]

And so, Lord, you who can add understanding to faith, allow me (to the extent that it is good for me) to understand that you exist as I believe you to exist and that you are what I believe you are. I believe you are *something than which nothing greater can be thought of [aliquid quo nihil maius cogitari possit]*.[4] Is it possible that nothing like that exists? After all, "the fool has said in his heart 'there is no God'" (Psalms 14:1 and 53:1). But when this fool hears the words "something than which nothing greater can be thought of," he must understand what

---

[1]From the Preface.

[2]From Chapter 1.

[3]Chapter 2.

[4]Or "that than which nothing greater can be conceived."

72

he hears; and what he understands then exists in his mind [*in intellectu eius est*], even if he doesn't think that such a being exists in fact. For there is a big difference between something existing [as an idea] in someone's mind and . . . that thing's existing in reality. When a painter first imagines what he is going to paint, he has it in his mind; but, since he has not yet made the painting itself, he doesn't think that it exists yet. Once he has made the painting, however, he not only has the idea of it in his mind, but he also knows that the painting itself exists in fact . . . .

So even a fool would have to admit that *something than which nothing greater can be thought of* exists [as an idea] in his mind since he understands this phrase when he hears it, and whatever is understood exists at least in the understanding (or mind). But here's my main point: *Something than which nothing greater can be thought of* cannot exist *only* [as an idea] in the mind because, in addition to existing [as an idea] in the mind, it can also be thought of as existing in reality [that is, objectively], which is greater [than existing only as an idea in the mind]. If *something than which nothing greater can be thought of* exists only as an idea in the mind, then "that than which something greater *cannot* be thought of" is "that than which something greater *can* be thought of," which is impossible [because it is self-contradictory]. Therefore, it necessarily follows that *something than which nothing greater can be thought of* must exist, not only as an idea in the mind, but in reality.

The nonexistence of God is impossible[1]

Furthermore, *something than which nothing greater can be thought of* so certainly exists that it is impossible to think that it doesn't exist. It is possible to think of *something that cannot be thought not to exist* [that is, a *necessary* being], and such a being would be greater than

---

[1]Chapter 3.

73

something that *can* be thought not to exist [that is, a *contingent* being]. If *something than which nothing greater can be thought of* could be thought of as not existing, then *something than which nothing greater can be thought of* would not be *something than which nothing greater can be thought of*, which is an outright contradiction and thus absurd. Therefore, *something than which nothing greater can be thought of* has such a high degree of existence [that is, necessary existence] that it cannot be thought of as not existing [that is, its nonexistence is *impossible*].

And you are this being, Oh Lord our God. You exist so truly . . . that you cannot be even *thought of* as not existing. And this is appropriate, for if the human mind could conceive of something greater than you, then a creature would rise above its creator and pass judgment on him, which is utterly absurd. Now, everything that exists, other than you alone, can be thought of as not existing. [That is, nothing else can be thought of as *something than which nothing greater can be thought of*.] You alone among all things have the truest and greatest degree of existence [necessary existence]; nothing else has that kind of existence [that is, everything else that exists has only contingent existence].

Why, then, has the fool said in his heart "there is no God," when it is obvious to a rational mind that you of all things exist to the highest possible extent [that is, necessarily]? It is because he is stupid and foolish.

How can anyone deny or doubt the existence of God?[1]

But how can a fool say in his heart what he cannot think? Or how could he not think what he says in his heart since "saying in one's

---

[1] Chapter 4.

74

heart" is the same as "thinking"? If (or *since*) the fool has thought this because he has said it in his heart *and* did *not* say it in his heart because he could *not* think it, then there must be two different ways in which something can be "said in the heart" or "thought." (1) In one sense, to think of something is to understand the word that stands for that thing. (2) In another sense, thinking of something is to understand the true nature (or essence) of the thing. God can be thought not to exist in the first sense, but not at all in the second sense. No one who understands what God is can doubt or deny that God exists. But someone might say "in his heart" that "God does not exist" because he fails to give these words any meaning or because he gives them some mistaken meaning. For God is *something than which nothing greater can be thought of.* Whoever grasps the true meaning of these words will then know that God exists in such a way that his nonexistence is unthinkable[1] and therefore impossible . . . .

I thank you, gracious Lord, I thank you! What I have believed on faith through your grace I now understand through your illumination, so that, even if I were not willing to *believe on faith* that you exist, I would *know* [on the basis of logic and reason] that you do . . . .

_____

[1]That is, inconceivable.

75

THOMAS AQUINAS
(1224-1274 AD)

from the

SUMMA THEOLOGICA[1]

The Existence of God

The existence of God is not self-evident[2]

There are those who claim that the existence of God is self-evident [which I myself do not believe]. One view here is that we have inborn knowledge of certain . . . self-evident truths [for example, if the statement "P" is true, then the statement "not-P" must be false]; and according to St. John of Damascus, "the knowledge of God is naturally

---

[1]Translated, paraphrased, and edited by George Cronk, © 1996. Aquinas's *Summa Theologica* is a massive theological and philosophical work, originally composed in Latin. Only one small part of the *Summa*, Part I, Question 2, "The Existence of God," is included in the present translation. For the Latin text, together with a standard English translation by Timothy McDermott, see St. Thomas Aquinas, *Summa Theologiae*, Volume 2 (on the "Existence and Nature of God") (New York: Blackfriars in conjunction with McGraw-Hill Book Company, 1964), pp. 4-17.

[2]Part I, Question 2, Article 1.

77

implanted in all people." Therefore, some say that the existence of God is self-evident.

Another argument for the self-evidence of God's existence is that some statements are seen to be self-evident as soon as we know the meanings of the terms used in such statements . . . . For example, once we understand what a whole is and what a part is, it is immediately obvious (self-evident) that a whole is larger than any one of its own parts. There are some [such as Anselm of Canterbury] who argue that as soon as the meaning of the word "God" is understood, it is then self-evident that God exists. For the word "God" means "something than which nothing greater can be thought of," and that which exists not only mentally but also in fact is greater than that which exists only mentally . . . . Thus, the proposition "God exists" is self-evidently true.

A third argument is based on the premise that the existence of truth is self-evident, since whoever denies the existence of truth is asserting that "truth does not exist," and, if truth does not exist, then the proposition "truth does not exist" must be true. Now, if anything is true, then truth must exist. But God is truth itself, since Jesus, according to the Gospel of John, said "I am the way, the truth, and the life" (John 4:6). So it follows that the existence of God is self-evident.

Against the foregoing arguments, it is said that no one can think the opposite of what is self-evident . . . . But there are people who assert the opposite of the statement "God exists": "The fool has said in his heart, there is no God" (Psalm 53:1). Therefore, the existence of God is *not* self-evident.

My own view is that something can be self-evident in two different ways: (1) self-evident *in itself*, but not *to us*; and (2) self-evident in itself *and* to us. A statement is self-evident when its predicate is part of the meaning of its subject. An example is the statement "a human being is an animal" because "animal" is part of the definition of "human being." If the meanings of the predicate and subject are known to all, the truth of the statement will be self-evident to all . . . . But if there are those who do not understand the meanings of the predicate and the subject, then the statement will be self-evident *in itself* but not self-evident to those who are ignorant of the meanings of the predicate and subject terms . . . .

As I see it, the statement "God exists" is self-evident *in itself* because the predicate is the same as the subject, that is, God is His own existence, as we will prove later on.[1] However, *since we cannot know the essence of God*, the claim that "God exists" is not self-evident *to us*, but rather needs to be proved from things that are more familiar to us . . . , that is, from effects [or events in the world] . . . . [see the following sections]

Although the existence of God is not self-evident, it can be proved[2]

[As usual, I will summarize the views of those who disagree with me before I present my own arguments.] Many deny that the existence of God can be proved. For example, (1) there are those who say that the existence of God is accepted on the basis of faith and that beliefs based on faith cannot be proved because proof results in knowledge rather than faith, which is of the unseen [not the knowable] . . . . (2) Others claim that . . . we cannot know what God *is* but only what He is *not* . . . . (3) And still others argue as follows: If God's existence could be proved, it could only be from His effects. But God's effects are not perfectly reflective of Him since He is infinite and His effects are finite (and there is no good comparison between the finite and the infinite).

---

[1] In Part I, Question 3, Article 4, which is not included in this translation.

[2] Part I, Question 2, Article 2.

79

Thus, since a cause cannot be proved by an effect that does not accurately reflect it, it seems that God's existence cannot be proved.

Contrary to these views, St. Paul says that "the invisible qualities of God are clearly seen and understood by the things that God has created" (Romans 1:20). This would not be true if God's existence could not be proved from the things that God has created, for knowing that a thing exists is the first step toward understanding it.

In my view, there are two kinds of proof: (1) from cause to effect, which explains *why* the effect exists; and (2) from effect to cause, which shows *that* the cause exists. When an effect is better known to us than its cause, we must reason from effect to cause in order to increase our knowledge of the cause; and from any effect the existence of its . . . cause may be proved, provided that the effect is well known to us. After all, isn't it obvious that, since an effect depends on its cause, if the effect exists then its cause must pre-exist it? Therefore, the existence of God, although it is not self-evident to us, can be proved from those of His effects that are known to us.

On this basis, I would now like to reply to those (cited above) who claim that the existence of God cannot be proved. (1) [Some] beliefs about the existence and nature of God are not only articles of faith, but can be proved through natural reason . . . . However, if someone cannot understand a proof, there is no reason why such a person cannot accept on faith something that can be proved and known [even though he himself cannot prove or know it]. (2) When the existence of a cause is proved from its effects, we do not know the essence of the cause but only its existence [that is, we don't know *what* it is, but only *that* it is] . . . . (3) I admit that an effect that only imperfectly reflects its cause cannot give us perfect knowledge of that cause. Nonetheless, we can know that the cause *exists* if we know that its effects exist. Thus, we can prove the *existence* of God from His

80

effects, even though, on the basis of such effects, we cannot perfectly know God's *inner essence* or true nature.

God exists[1]

[I think that God exists, and I also think that I can prove it.] There are two major objections to my view. First, . . . if one of two contraries is infinite, then the other can have no existence. Now, God is infinitely good. So, if God existed, the existence of evil, which is the opposite of goodness, would be impossible. However, there is evil in the world. Therefore, God does not exist. (In opposition to this view, I quote St. Augustine, who said, "Since God is supremely good, He would not allow any evil to exist unless He were able to bring good even out of evil." In His infinite goodness, God allows evil to exist in order to produce good from it.)[2]

The second objection is as follows: It is unnecessary to assume that what can be explained by a few causes has been produced by many. But it seems that everything in the world can be explained without reference to God. All natural phenomena can be explained by natural causes; and all voluntary events can be traced back to human reason or will. Therefore, there is no need to assume the existence of God [in order to explain what is happening in the universe]. (My reply to this is that nature produces definite effects under the direction of a higher agent, and therefore all natural events must be traced back to God as the first cause of nature. Similarly, voluntary occurrences must be traced back to some cause higher than human reason or will since these can

---

[1]Part I, Question 2, Article 3.

[2]The passage in parentheses is Aquinas's "Reply to Objection 1," which is located in traditional editions at the end of Part I, Question 2, Article 3.

81

change or cease to exist. All things that are changeable and capable of going out of existence must be traced back to an unchangeable and self-necessary first cause . . . [as will be shown below]. [In other words, the very existence of both natural and human causes must be explained by reference to a more fundamental, first, cause.])[1]

Against these arguments, we note that the Bible reports that God has said, "I am who am" (Exodus 3:14). And I will now show that the existence of God can be proved in five ways.[2]

(1) The argument from change

The first and most obvious way is the argument from change. Our senses show, and there is no doubt, that some of the things in the world are changing. Now, whatever changes must be caused to change by something other than itself. (Nothing can change unless it has the *potential* to be that into which it changes, whereas something that causes change must *actually be* what it is causing something else to change into. [In other words,] to cause change is to draw something out of potentiality into actuality, and this can be done only by something that is already in actuality. For example, fire, which is actually hot, can cause wood, which is potentially hot, to become actually hot, thereby causing change in the wood. Now, something cannot simultaneously be both actually and potentially X, although it can be actually X and potentially Y at the same time. Something that is actually hot is

---

[1]The passage in parentheses is Aquinas's "Reply to Objection 2," which is located in traditional editions at the end of Part I, Question 2, Article 3.

[2]For a sympathetic and illuminating interpretation of Aquinas's five proofs, see F.C. Copleston, *Aquinas* (New York: Penguin Books, 1955), pp. 114-130.

potentially cold, but nothing can be both actually and potentially hot at the same time. Therefore, it is impossible for something that changes to be the cause of that change; that is, something that changes cannot change itself. Thus, [to repeat what we stated above,] whatever is changing must be caused to change by something other than itself.)[1] If anything that changes must be caused to change by something other than itself, then that cause is itself caused by still another cause, and so on. But this process of cause and effect cannot go on to infinity because, if it did, there would be no first cause of change and thus no later causes of change (since later causes of change are merely the effects of a first or primary cause -- for example, a stick can move something only if the stick is moved by a hand). Therefore, there must be a first cause of change, which itself is not caused or changed by anything, and this everyone understands to be "God."

(2) The argument from causation

The second way to prove the existence of God is from the fact of . . . causation. In the world that we perceive with our senses, we find a series of . . . causes. Nothing can be the . . . cause of itself, for then it would be prior to itself, which is impossible. It is also impossible for a series of . . . causes to go on to infinity. In every series of . . . causes, the first cause produces one or more later causes, and the later causes produce the last event in the series. If a . . . cause were removed from the series, so would its effect be removed. Thus, if there were no first cause [in a series of causes], that is, if the series went on to infinity, there could be no later . . . causes and no last event in the series.

---

[1]The passage in parentheses is an argument within the main argument. It is an attempt to prove Aquinas's claim that "whatever changes must be caused to change by something other than itself."

But it is obvious that there are such causes and events. So there must be a first . . . cause, which everyone calls "God."

(3) The argument from contingency

The third proof of God's existence is based on the distinction between possibility and necessity . . . . There are things that can either exist or not [that is, *contingent beings*], which is clear from the fact that some things come into being and later pass out of existence (that is, they exist at some times but not at others). But something like this [a contingent being] cannot always exist because something whose nonexistence is possible must have not-existed at some time. So if everything can not-be [that is, if everything has contingent existence], then at some time before now there would have been absolutely *nothing* in existence. But if this were the case, then even now there would be nothing in existence because something that doesn't exist can begin to exist only if it is brought into existence by something already existing. If at some time before now there was nothing in existence, it would have been impossible for anything to begin to exist and there would be nothing existing now, which is obviously false. Thus, it can't be that *everything's* existence is merely possible [contingent]. There must be something that has *necessary* existence . . . . Therefore, we must admit the existence of a being that exists necessarily . . . [and this everyone calls "God"].

(4) The argument from degrees of perfection

The fourth proof is derived from the gradations that are observed in the world. Some things seem to be better, more true, more noble than other things. But something can have "more" or "less" of a quality only if it is closer to or further away from the maximum of that quality. For example, the hotter something is, the closer it is to that which is maximally hot. So there must be something that is maximally true, good, noble, and this must be the greatest conceivable being. As

84

Aristotle says in Chapter 2 of his **Metaphysics**, whatever is greatest in truth is greatest in being. In the same book, Aristotle also says that the maximum in any category is the cause of everything else in that category (for example, fire, being the hottest thing [or stuff] [in existence] must be the cause of all heat [?]). Therefore, there must be something that is the cause of the existence, goodness, and all other perfections of things in the world, and this we call "God."

(5) The argument from design

The fifth proof of God's existence follows from the way things happen in the world. Even things that lack consciousness, such as physical objects, tend toward an end. In fact, they always (or almost always) behave in such a way as to produce what is best [with regard to the natural order]. This shows that things in nature reach their end, not by chance or accident, but by design. But anything that lacks consciousness can tend toward an end [or follow a design] only if it is directed to do so by some other being that is conscious and intelligent (as an arrow is directed toward a target by an archer). It follows that there is some intelligent being who directs all things in nature toward their end, and this being we call "God."[1]

---

[1]Aquinas's **Summa Theologica** (**ST**) was written between 1265 and 1272 and was left unfinished. In an earlier work, the **Summa Contra Gentiles** (**SCG**) (composed between 1259 and 1264), he says that all things in nature tend to cooperate in the production and maintenance of a single and stable cosmic order. This, it seems, is the "end" pursued "even by things that lack consciousness." Aquinas also says in the **SCG** that such things could not "tend to [such] a definite end" unless they were directed thereto by "some [intelligent] being by whose providence the world is governed," that is, by God. **SCG**, Book I, Chapter 13, ¶ 35.

RENÉ DESCARTES
(1596-1650 AD)

from the

MEDITATIONS ON FIRST PHILOSOPHY[1]

Meditation I: On Those Things That Can Be Called into Doubt

Several years ago, I realized that I had accepted many false beliefs when I was young and that I had built many of my later beliefs on those early false beliefs, so that my later beliefs were therefore doubtful because of their weak foundations. I also realized that, in order to establish a firm basis for knowledge, I would have to demolish the overall structure of my beliefs and start over again from new foundations. But that task seemed so enormous that I decided to wait until a point in my life when I would be best able to undertake

---

[1]Translated, paraphrased, and edited by George Cronk. © 1996. Descartes' *Meditations* was written in Latin between 1638 and 1640 and originally published in 1641 under the title, *Meditationes de prima Philosophia*. A corrected second edition of the work, which is considered the standard text, was published in 1642. See René Descartes, *Meditationes de prima Philosophia* (a bilingual edition), ed. George Heffernan (Notre Dame: University of Notre Dame Press, 1990). With Descartes' approval, the *Meditations* was translated from Latin into French by Louis-Charles d'Albert, Duc de Luynes, and published in 1647 as *Les méditations métaphysiques touchant la première philosophie*. See René Descartes, *Méditations Métaphysiques*, ed. André Robinet (Paris: Librarie Philosophique J. VRIN, 1976).

the job I had set for myself. Now, however, I think that I have waited long enough. I must get to it before it is too late. Today, then, having freed my mind of worry and having arranged for some peace and quiet, I am here in solitude, ready at last to work on the demolition of all my beliefs and opinions.

Descartes' program of radical doubt

To accomplish my task, I don't need to show that each and every one of my beliefs is false. I may never be able to do that. However, reason advises me to adopt the following policy: *I will treat any belief that is to the slightest extent uncertain and subject to doubt just as though it is obviously false.* On this basis, I will be able to reject any belief that is at all doubtful. [And I will accept only those beliefs that are completely certain and indubitable.][1]

Furthermore, in order to complete this demolition project, I don't think that I will have to examine all of my beliefs and opinions one by one -- another task that might be endless. Instead, I will work on the *foundations* of my current and former beliefs, for if I can undermine those foundations then the entire building erected on them will collapse. So let's look at the underlying principles on which my beliefs and opinions have rested.

───────────────

[1]In the *Discourse on Method* (1637), Descartes describes his epistemological strategy as follows: "[B]ecause I wanted to concentrate completely on the search for truth, I thought I ought to do just the opposite, that is, reject as being absolutely false any belief for which I could find even the slightest reason for doubt, in order to see if, after that, there did not remain anything in the belief which was entirely indubitable." See *Discourse on Method and Meditations on First Philosophy*, trans. Donald A. Cress (Indianapolis: Hackett Publishing Company, 1980), p. 17.

Sense experience

[One such underlying principle is sensation, or sense experience.] In the past, I thought that beliefs I held to be true were learned either from or through the senses [of sight, smell, hearing, taste, and touch]. Now, however, I recall that my senses have at least occasionally deceived me [for example, I have taken a rock perceived from a distance to be an animal], and it would seem prudent never to completely trust those who have misled us even once.

Nonetheless, although my senses may deceive me about things that are small or far away, there may still be beliefs based on perception that I cannot possibly doubt, for example, that I am here, sitting in front of the fire, wearing a dressing gown, holding this piece of paper [that I am writing on], and so on. Also, is it possible to doubt or deny that my hands and the other parts of my body exist?

Insanity and Dreaming

Of course, there are insane people whose brains are so diseased that they are convinced that they are kings when they are paupers, or that they are finely dressed when in fact they are completely naked, or that their heads are made of clay, or that they are gourds, or that they are made of glass. But these people are out of their minds, and I would appear to be just as crazy if I were to take them as an example for myself.

But what about sleeping and dreaming? When I dream, I often have experiences that are at least as strange as the experiences of crazy people when they are awake. Also, quite often in my dreams I have been convinced that I am here before the fire, wearing my dressing gown, etc., when in fact I am undressed and in bed!

That said, it still seems obvious to me that I am now completely awake, looking at this piece of paper, shaking my head (which is not heavy with sleep), reaching out with my hands and touching the things around me. None of the things I am now perceiving would be so *distinct* if I were asleep and dreaming. And yet, I must admit that I have often been deceived by similar experiences in my dreams! When I think about this problem very carefully and critically, it seems to me at this point that there are *no completely reliable signs by which I can distinguish clearly between dreaming and waking states* . . . . [which is a rather shocking realization].

So let's assume that I am now dreaming. Imagine that my eyes are closed, that my head is not moving, that I am not extending my hands. Indeed, let us imagine that I do not have any hands, or even a body! Even then, it would seem that the things I experience in my dreams are like painted images, which must be representations of real things, so that things like eyes, heads, hands, and bodies are "really real" and not just imaginary. After all, when painters try to represent things like sirens and satyrs[1] in especially bizarre ways, they cannot give them utterly new natures; they simply put together the parts of various known animals. Even if a painter were to depict something so novel that no one had ever seen anything like it (that is, something completely fictitious and unreal), nonetheless the colors used by the painter would have to be real.

Similarly, while things like eyes, heads, hands, and the like may be imaginary, one must acknowledge the reality of certain more simple

---

[1]In Greek and Roman mythology, a siren is a sea nymph, part bird and part woman, who lures sailors to their deaths on rock coasts by seductive singing; and a satyr is a rowdy and lecherous god of the forest having pointed ears and short horns, the head and body of a man, and the legs of a goat.

90

and universal things, from which . . . our mental images of things like eyes, heads, and hands are constructed. Things of this sort seem to include *matter* and its *extension* [in space], the *shape* of extended things, their *quantity* or *number*, their *size*, the *places* in which they stand, the *time* through which they exist, and so forth.

Perhaps . . . physics, astronomy, medicine, and other sciences that study composite things [that is, things made up of various parts] are subject to doubt, but sciences like arithmetic and geometry, which study only the most simple and most general things [numbers, triangles, etc.] and which are unconcerned with whether such things actually exist, may give us knowledge that is certain and beyond doubt. After all, whether I am awake or dreaming, two plus three always equals five, and a square never has more [or less] than four sides. It seems impossible to think that such obvious [mathematical] truths might be false or in any way uncertain.

A deceptive God?

However, I hold the traditional view that a God exists who is all-powerful and that this God has created me as I am. Isn't it possible that, although there is in fact no earth, no sky, no physical objects, no shape, no size, and no place, God makes it *seem* to me that such things exist? I believe that other people are sometimes mistaken in what they take to be obviously true. Isn't it possible that *I* am wrong when I add two and three, or count the sides of a square, or make judgments about even more simple things (if there is anything simpler)?

Many, of course, will deny that God would deceive me since He is thought to be all-good; but if God's goodness is inconsistent with His allowing me to be always deceived, it seems just as inconsistent with

91

God's goodness that he would allow me to be deceived at all (that is, even once in a while), and yet I *am* sometimes deceived . . . !¹

So I feel compelled to admit that none of my former beliefs is beyond doubt; and I am not saying this thoughtlessly or carelessly, but on the basis of well thought out arguments. Therefore, since all of my former beliefs are subject to doubt, I must refuse to accept them just as I would if they were obviously false. I must make a concerted effort to do this if I am to arrive at anything that is certain . . . .

The demon hypothesis

In carrying out my project here, I will not assume (as suggested above) that God, who is all-good and the source of all truth, causes me to be deceived in my beliefs. Rather, my hypothesis is this: There is an overwhelmingly powerful and clever evil spirit (demon) who does everything he can to deceive me. I will assume that the sky, the air, the earth, colors, shapes, sounds, and all other external things [that is, things that apparently exist outside of my mind] are nothing but figments of my dreams, used by the demon to fool me. I will view myself as having no hands, no eyes, no flesh, no blood, and no senses, but as having the false belief that I possess all these things. I will consistently and firmly hold onto these assumptions so that, even if it is beyond my ability to grasp anything true, I will at least be able [by suspending my judgment] to avoid any false beliefs that the powerful and clever demon may try to get me to accept . . . .

---

¹Descartes returns to this issue in the fourth meditation. See p. 111, below.

Meditation II: On the Human Mind, Which is Better Known Than the Body

The first meditation has thrown me into such great doubts that I cannot forget them, nor can I see how to resolve them. I am in great confusion. It's as though I had fallen into a whirlpool and can neither touch the bottom with my foot nor swim up to the top. But I am determined to work my way out of this. I will continue to follow the path I started on in the first meditation, that is, I will reject anything that is subject to even the slightest degree of doubt, treating it as though it were absolutely false; and I will persist in this until I find something certain -- or at least until I know for certain that nothing is certain . . . .

The existence of the self

I will assume, therefore, that everything I see is unreal. I will refuse to trust my memory and will deny that anything it calls to mind ever actually happened. I will force myself to think that I have no senses and that my body and its shape, extension, movement, and place are illusions. What then will be certain? Perhaps nothing but this: that nothing in the world is certain.

But how do I know that there is nothing other than the things I have just listed? Might there be something else that exists beyond doubt? What about God . . . ? Doesn't he put my thoughts into my mind? Not necessarily. Perhaps I myself am the author of my own thoughts. But then wouldn't I be something? I am assuming that I have no senses and no body. But what follows from that? Am I so connected to my body and my senses that I could not exist without them? But I have convinced myself that there is nothing whatsoever in the world -- no sky, no earth, no minds, no bodies. Doesn't it follow from this that I do not exist?

And yet, if I have convinced myself of something, then I would have to exist [in order to do the convincing and in order to be convinced]. Now, I have also hypothesized [at the end of the first meditation] that there is an extremely powerful and sly deceiver [or demon], who tries everything to deceive me and to keep me deceived. But here's the thing: *If I am deceived, then I must exist!*[1] No matter how much the demonic deceiver deceives me, he can never cause me to be nothing while I am in a position to think that I am something. So all things considered, I must conclude that the statement "I am, I exist" must be true whenever I say it or think it.

The mind-body problem

Now I know *that* I exist, but I do not yet know *what* I am. And I must from now on be careful not to take myself to be something other than I really am and thus be mistaken in the knowledge that I consider to be the most certain and evident. Therefore, I will review the beliefs about myself that I held before I began these meditations. And again, I will reject anything that is at all doubtful on the basis of what I set forth in the first meditation, so that nothing will remain except that which is certain and beyond doubt.

What, then, did I used to believe I am? A human being, of course. But what is that? Perhaps I should say a rational animal. But no, for then I would have to go into the meanings of "animal" and

---

[1]In the **Discourse on Method**, Descartes penned the famous slogan, "*Cogito, ergo sum,*" which in Latin means "I think, therefore I am." See **Discourse on Method and Meditations on First Philosophy**, trans. Donald A. Cress (Indianapolis: Hackett Publishing Company, 1980), p. 17. Here, in the **Meditations**, he is saying that if he is deceived, which is a form of thinking, he must exist.

"rational," so that from one question, I will gradually slide into many more difficult ones. I just don't have enough time for that. I want to concentrate on my former beliefs about myself and my nature. Naturally, I thought that I have a face, hands, arms, and all the other physical parts (also found in a corpse) that I referred to collectively as "body." I also believed that I eat, walk, have sensations, and think -- and I believed that these actions were caused by my soul. As for the nature of the soul, either I did not think about it at all or I considered it to be a subtle air, fire, or ether flowing through my bodily organism.

With regard to physical objects, I had no doubts; I believed that I knew their nature. I thought of physical objects this way: A physical object has a shape and occupies a place; it fills a space so as to exclude other objects from that space; it can be perceived through the five senses; it can be moved in various ways, not by itself, but by other things that cause it to move by touching it. Furthermore, I believed that the powers of self-movement, sensation, and thinking did not belong to the nature of physical objects, and I was surprised to find that such powers *are* found in certain bodies [for example, in a human body].

But now, assuming that a powerful and evil deceiver is continually using all his resources to deceive me, what can I say about myself? Can I say that I have any of the characteristics that I have attributed to physical objects? After reflection, I can find no physical qualities that are essential to myself . . . .

What about the qualities I earlier assigned to the soul? As for eating or moving about, these must be illusions if I have no body. It would appear that sensation, too, cannot go on without a body, and, furthermore, I seem to have sensed many things in dreams that I later realized I did not really perceive.

95

Thinking as the essence of the self

But then I come to thinking. *This*, I believe, really does belong to my nature. This alone cannot be separated from me. I am; I exist; this is beyond doubt. But for how long do I exist? So long as I think. For all I know, it may be that, if I stopped thinking completely, I would cease to exist completely. I am not now accepting anything that is not true beyond all doubt. Therefore, as far as I know with *certainty*, I am *a thing that thinks*, that is, a mind, or soul, or intellect, or reason[1] -- words whose meanings I have not understood until now. I know that I am a real, existing thing. But what kind of thing? As I have said already: *a thing that thinks*.

What else am I . . . ? I am not the collection of physical organs called the human body. Nor am I some elusive air flowing through these organs -- neither wind, nor fire, nor vapor, nor breath, for I am still assuming that no such things exist. And yet, I *am* something! Perhaps the things I am assuming to be unreal [the body, etc.] (because I am not certain of their existence) are in fact identical with myself. I don't know, and I'm not going to argue about it now. I can argue only on the basis of what I am certain of. I am certain that I exist, and I am asking what *is* this "I" that I know to exist?

It is clear that knowing the true nature of myself does not depend on anything I do not yet know to exist. Thus, it does not depend on anything of which I can form a mental image . . . , for having a mental image is nothing but the contemplation of the shape or image of a physical object. I know for certain that I exist, and I also know that all mental images, including everything associated with the nature of

---

[1]Latin version: *"mens, sive animus, sive intellectus, sive ratio"*; French version: *"un esprit, un entendement ou une raison"*.

96

physical objects, may be nothing but dreams . . . . Thus, I know that nothing that I can think about with the assistance of mental images is relevant to my knowledge of myself, and I must insistently withdraw my mind from the products of imagination if it is to grasp its own nature as distinctly as possible.

Then what am I? A thing that thinks. And what is that? A thing that doubts, understands, affirms, denies, wills, refuses, and which also imagines and has sensations . . . . Am I not now doubting almost everything, understanding a few things, affirming that some things are true, denying other things, desiring [willing] to know more, refusing to be deceived? Isn't it true that I form mental images of many things (even against my will) and that I perceive many things through my senses . . . ? Are any of these things [doubting, understanding, etc.] distinct from my thinking? Are any separate from my nature? It is so obvious that it is I who doubt, I who understand, I who will -- I don't see how this could be any more obvious . . . . [It is also I who have mental images and sensations. And even though the objects that appear through imagination and sensation are not real, nonetheless, I have mental images and sense experiences as parts of my thinking . . . .]

Meditation III: On the Existence of God

I will now close my eyes, plug my ears, withdraw my senses from their objects, and remove from my mind all images of physical objects (or, because it may be impossible to remove all physical images, I will treat them as empty and false). Conversing only with myself and looking deeply into myself, I will try to gain a better knowledge of my nature. I am a thinking thing -- a being who doubts, affirms, denies, knows some things and is ignorant of many, wills, refuses, and also imagines and senses. As I stated in the second meditation, even if the things I imagine and sense have no real existence outside me,

97

nonetheless I am certain that sensations and mental images exist in me at least as aspects of my thinking.

The search for clear and distinct ideas

I have now summed up all that I really know, or at least all that I am aware that I know. Now I will look more closely to see whether there are other things about myself that I have not yet noticed. I am certain that I am a thing that thinks. From this, can't I figure out what is needed to make me certain of other things? In my knowledge of myself as a thinking thing, there is only a clear and distinct grasp of what I see about myself, and this would not give me certainty [as it does] if it should ever happen that something I see clearly and distinctly turns out to be false. So it seems that I can bank on the general rule that everything that I can clearly and distinctly grasp is true.

But in the past, I accepted many beliefs that I thought were completely obvious, only to find out later on that they were doubtful. These were ideas about the earth, the sky, the stars, and other things perceived through the senses. But what was really clear about these objects? Only that I had ideas of them in my mind, and even now some of these ideas are in my mind. And there was something else I believed to be perfectly clear, which is not in fact perfectly clear, namely, (1) that there are things outside myself [such as physical objects], (2) that these external things cause my ideas of those things to be in my mind, and (3) that the ideas perfectly resemble the things themselves. Either I was mistaken about that, or, if I was right, it was not because my beliefs on this matter were supported by good reasons or evidence.

But what follows from that? When I focused on very simple and easy matters in arithmetic or geometry -- for example, that two plus three equals five -- weren't they clear enough to allow me to know that they were true? But later [as stated in the first meditation], I came to doubt even such simple truths because it seemed possible that God might have given me a nature that could deceive me about the most obvious things. For whenever I think of an all-powerful God, I realize that, if He wanted to, He could cause me to be mistaken even about those things I think I see with complete clarity.

Yet when I turn to those things that seem most clear to me, I am so completely convinced that they are real that I impulsively exclaim as follows: "Let anyone deceive me as much as he can. Nonetheless, he will never be able to make me not exist as long as I think that I do exist, nor will he be able make it true that I never existed since it is true that I exist now, nor will he be able to make two plus three equal either more or less than five, nor will he be able to make something else true in which I can see an obvious contradiction" [for example, "X is a triangle, and X has four sides"].

Furthermore, I have no reason to think that God is such a deceiver. In fact, I don't even know yet whether God exists! So the suspicion that God may be continually deceiving me is very . . . weak. However, to remove these doubts, I must, as soon as possible, try to determine (1) *whether or not God exists* and (2) *whether or not He can be a deceiver*. Until I know these two things, I will never be certain of anything else . . . .

Ideas of external objects

But for the moment, I want to return to those of my ideas that I believe to be caused by things existing outside myself [for example, physical objects]. Why should I believe that these ideas resemble those objects? First, I have a strong natural impulse to believe it. Second, I find that these ideas arise in my mind independently of my will; in fact, they often appear when I don't want them to. For example, right now, I am feeling heat whether I want to or not, and I therefore believe that this sensation is coming from something other than myself, namely, the fire that I am now sitting next to. It also seems obvious that an external object [like the fire here] impresses its own likeness upon my senses . . . .

But are these reasons good enough? When I say that I have a natural impulse to believe something, that is not the same thing as saying that reason reveals the thing's truth to me . . . . When reason reveals something to me (for example, that from the fact that I doubt it follows that I exist), that thing is completely beyond doubt . . . . But my natural impulses very often drive me to act against my better judgment, for example, in decisions about what is good, so I can't see why I should trust them on matters having to do with truth and falsity.

The fact that my ideas of external objects are independent of my will does not prove that they necessarily come from things outside myself. Many of the natural impulses I have just spoken of are often in conflict with my will. Furthermore, there may be within me some other not yet discovered ability that produces these ideas; for example, such ideas [of tables, houses, etc.] come to me in dreams when the objects dreamed of are not present.

Moreover, even if my ideas of external objects are caused by such objects, it does not follow that the ideas must accurately resemble the objects. Indeed, it frequently seems that ideas differ greatly from their objects. For example, I have two different ideas about [the size of] the sun. One such idea is based on sense experience . . . . I perceive the sun to be very small. My other idea is derived from the science of astronomy, which tells me . . . that the sun is many times larger than the earth. Both of these ideas cannot be correct likenesses of the sun (assuming that it exists outside of myself), and I am convinced by reason that the idea based on sense experience is the one most likely to be false.

Therefore, it would appear that my belief that there are things outside myself that send their likenesses to me through my sense organs is based, not on certain judgment, but rather on blind impulse.

Ideas and their causes

However, there may be another way to find out whether my ideas of external objects come from things that really exist outside me. Insofar as ideas of external things are just . . . thoughts, they are all the same, that is, they all arise in my mind in the same way. But different ideas present different things to me, and there are great differences between the things thus presented. Isn't it obvious that those ideas that present *substances* to me represent something "more real" than those ideas that represent only *modes* or *accidents* [of substances]?[1] And the idea by which I understand . . . God (that is, eternal, infinite, all-knowing, all-powerful, and creator of all things other than Himself) represents "more reality" than those ideas that present only finite substances to me.

Now, reason shows that *there must be at least as much reality in a cause as there is in its effect.* Where could an effect get its reality if

---

[1]For Descartes, a *substance* is "that which can exist by itself" without the aid of any other thing. A substance must be distinguished from its *accidents* and *modes* [of existence]. Descartes seems to use the term *accident* for the characteristics (properties, qualities, or attributes) that may be predicated of a substance. For example, an apple is a substance, and redness might be one of its accidents. The word *mode* refers to a substance's "manner of existence," that is, the *way* in which a substance exists (if at all). The existence of some things -- for example, apples -- is *both possible and actual*; other things, such as unicorns, have *possible but not actual* existence; the existence of round squares, four-sided triangles, brothers with no siblings, and so forth, is *impossible*; and (according to Descartes and others) the existence of certain other things, especially God, is *necessary*.

not from its cause? And how can the cause give reality to its effect if the cause itself does not have that reality to give? It follows, then, that something cannot come into existence out of nothing, nor can something more perfect or more real come into existence from something less perfect or less real.

This is true, not only for effects that actually exist [in the external world], but also for ideas, which seem to have a merely subjective existence [in the mind]. Thus, a stone, which did not exist before, cannot come into existence now unless it is caused to exist by something else that contains everything . . . that is in the stone. And something that is not hot can be made hot only by something else that has at least as much heat in it as it transmits to the other . . . . [1] Further, I can have no idea of heat or of a stone unless the idea is caused by something having at least as much reality in it as I think is in the heat or in the stone . . . .

Since an idea is a subjective representation of one reality rather than another, the cause of the idea must have at least as much actual reality in it as the reality represented subjectively in the idea. Otherwise, we would have an idea with a content that was not in the cause of the idea, and we would then have to conclude that the idea got this content from nothing. Even though something appears in the mind only through an idea (which is subjective), it is not nothing and cannot come from nothing . . . . Although one idea may be caused by another

---

[1]Descartes' actual sentence reads, "*Et la chaleur ne peut être produite dans un sujet qui en était auparavant privé, si ce n'est par une chose qui soit d'un ordre, d'un degré ou d'un genre au moins aussi parfait que la chaleur, et ainsi des autres.*" A literal rendering of this would be, "And heat cannot be produced in a subject that was not hot previously if it isn't done by something of an order, degree, or type at least as perfect as the heat, and the same is true for the other things." I have translated this more loosely above.

idea, this can't go back to infinity. There must be a primary idea caused by an "archetype" containing actually or objectively all the reality that the idea contains subjectively. Reason shows that my ideas are like images that may fail to accurately represent the things from which they derive but that cannot contain anything greater or more perfect than is in the things themselves . . . .

From ideas and their causes to God

But where does all this take me? On the one hand, if one of my ideas has something in it that is not within myself, then I could not be the cause of that idea. The cause of the idea would have to be something other than myself, and it would then follow that I am not alone in the world. On the other hand, if I have no such ideas, then I will have no foolproof reason to believe that anything exists other than myself . . . .

In addition to my idea of myself . . . , I have ideas of God, lifeless physical objects, angels, animals, and other people. My ideas of *other people, animals, and angels* could be composed from my ideas of myself, physical objects, and God -- that is, even if no people (other than myself), animals, or angels existed, I could have ideas of these things.

But what about my ideas of *physical objects*? Again, it seems that I could be the sole author of such ideas . . . . I notice that there is very little in my ideas of physical objects that I can grasp clearly and distinctly. What I do see clearly and distinctly is that physical objects have size, length, breadth, depth, shape . . . , position (which things with shapes have in relation to one another), motion (which is alteration of position) . . . , substance, duration, and number.

The other qualities of physical objects -- light, color, sound, odor, taste, heat and cold and other tactile attributes -- are so confused and obscure that I can't be sure whether they exist or not, that is, whether my ideas of these qualities are of something or of nothing . . . . For example, the ideas I have of heat and cold are so unclear and indistinct that I cannot decide whether cold is only the absence of heat or vice versa, or whether both are real qualities, or whether neither exists at all. Since all ideas are ideas of something, and if cold is nothing but the absence of heat, then my idea of coldness, which represents something real and positive to me, may be called false [since it presents something as real and positive that is, in fact, neither real nor positive] . . . .

To explain the existence of my ideas of the ["secondary qualities"] of physical objects (light, color, sound, etc.), I do not need to assume any creator other than myself. I know by reason that, if even one of these ideas is false (that is, if it presents nothing as though it were something), then it proceeds from nothing, which would mean that such ideas are in me solely because of some deficiency in my nature (which is imperfect). However, if any such idea is true, I see no reason why I could not have produced it from myself -- for this kind of idea presents so little reality to me that I can't even distinguish it from nothing.

As for those qualities of physical objects that are clear and distinct (size, shape, position, etc.) ["primary qualities"], it seems that I could have borrowed some from my idea of myself, namely, substance, duration, number, and other things of this kind. I think of a stone as a substance (that is, something that can exist on its own) and I also think of myself as a substance. Although I recognize that I am a thing that thinks and not an extended (or material) thing and that a stone is an extended (or material) thing and not a thing that thinks (and that therefore the two ideas are quite different), nonetheless we are both

104

substances.[1] Further, I could have gotten the ideas of duration and number (which I apply to physical objects and other things) from thinking that I exist now and have existed for some time [duration] and that I have several thoughts and can count such thoughts [number]. It is true that extension, shape, position, and motion are not characteristics of my essence since I am nothing but a substance that thinks. However, since they are only ways in which a physical substance would exist, and since I myself *am* a substance [and therefore contain more, not less, reality than the *modes* of extension, shape, position, and motion], those qualities may be contained in me eminently.[2]

The existence of God -- the first argument

There remains *my idea of God*. Is there anything in this idea that could not have originated with me? By "God," I mean an infinite and independent substance, all-knowing and all-powerful, who created me and everything else (if, in fact, there is anything besides myself). The more I think about these features [of the divine nature], the less it seems that they could have been imagined by myself alone. From this it necessarily follows that God exists.

How so? Although I have the idea of substance because I myself am a substance, it is not the idea of an *infinite* substance. I could have no such idea from myself since I am a *finite* substance. The idea of

---

[1]For Descartes, an "extended" thing is something that occupies space. The mind is a thinking process and not a material object. Therefore, it does not occupy space, is not "extended." A stone, however, is a material thing that does occupy space and is thus "extended."

[2]For Descartes, a being can be an *eminent* cause when, as a cause, it has *more* reality in it than is in its effect.

infinite substance [which I have in my mind] must be caused by some substance that is actually infinite.

Someone might say that I have no true idea of infinity but only of an absence of limits, just as I understand rest as the absence of motion and darkness as the absence of light. But no, I clearly see that there is more reality in an infinite substance than there is in a finite one. So my concept of the infinite must somehow precede my idea of the finite, that is, my understanding of God precedes my understanding of myself.[1] How could I know that I doubt and desire, that I am deficient and imperfect, if I didn't already have the idea of something more perfect against which I could recognize my defects?

Also . . . , the idea of God cannot be thought . . . to come from nothing since it is completely clear and distinct and has more "reality content" than any other idea. For this reason, no idea is more true in itself or less likely to be false. The idea of a supremely perfect and infinite being is, I say, completely true. It may be possible to think that no such being exists, but it is not possible to think (as I did about the idea of coldness) that my idea of God is not an idea of something. This idea is clear and distinct to the highest degree. It contains everything else that I grasp clearly and distinctly, everything real and true, everything with any perfection.

It doesn't matter that I can't fully understand the infinite, that there are many aspects of God that I can't understand fully or even imagine. It is the nature of the infinite that the finite cannot understand it. It is sufficient that I understand this and realize that anything that . . . has any perfection (including countless things of which I may be

---

[1]Descartes seems to be saying that I could not understand the finite (that is, myself) if my mind did not first understand the nature of the infinite (that is, God).

106

ignorant) gets its perfection from God [since the imperfect can acquire perfection only from something that is already perfect]. I conclude that, of all my ideas, my idea of God is the most true, the most clear, and the most distinct.

But is it possible that I am greater than I have been assuming? Can all the perfections I attribute to God be in me potentially, even though they do not show themselves in actuality? I believe that my knowledge has been increasing, and I can see no obstacle to its increasing more and more, even to infinity. And if my knowledge were to increase to infinity, why couldn't I then acquire all the remaining perfections of God? Finally, if these perfections are already in me potentially, why couldn't this explain my idea of perfection?

None of that is on target. First, the gradual increase of my knowledge and the fact that I have potentialities that have not yet been actualized are not consistent with the idea of God. In God, there is no potential [since, as a perfect being, God is completely actualized]. As a matter of fact, the gradual increase of my knowledge makes it clear that I am imperfect [since it makes no sense to say that something perfect can be made *more* perfect]. Second, my knowledge, even if it continually increases, will never be infinite because it will never reach a point where it cannot be further increased. But God is actually infinite; nothing can be added to His perfection. Third, an idea of something cannot be produced by that which is potential (which is, strictly speaking, nothing); it must be produced by something that is actual.

Reason makes all of this obvious. It is when I am not paying close attention, and when the images of perceptible things get in the way of clear thinking, that I forget that the idea of a being more perfect than myself must proceed from a being that really is more perfect than I.

The existence of God -- the second argument

Now I must ask whether I who have this idea [of a perfect being] could exist if such a being did not exist. What causes me to exist? Myself? My parents? Other things less perfect than God? (For we cannot think of or imagine anything *more* perfect than or even *as* perfect as God.)

If I were the cause of my own existence, I would have no doubts, no unfulfilled desires, no defects; for I would have given myself all the perfections of which I have any idea. Thus, I would be God! The things I lack seem no more difficult to acquire than the things I have. It would have been much more difficult for me (a substance that thinks) to have come into being out of nothing than it would be to acquire the knowledge (just an attribute of a thinking substance) of the many things of which I am ignorant. Surely, if, in creating myself, I gave myself what is harder to get [that is, existence], I would have also given myself complete knowledge, which is easier to get [than being itself]. I would not have denied myself *any* of the perfections that are contained in my idea of God. None of these seems harder to acquire than being itself; and if any of them *were* harder to acquire than existence, then they would now appear so to me (on the assumption that I am my own creator) because I should then discover in them the limits of my power.

I can't get around the preceding argument by claiming that I have always existed as I do now and that therefore there is no point in looking for my creator. My lifetime can be divided up into countless parts, each of which is independent of the others. From the fact that I existed a short time ago, it does not follow that I must exist now. For me to exist at this moment, some cause must recreate me or keep me in existence from moment to moment. It is obvious to anyone who understands the nature of time that the same force and action are required to *preserve* the existence of something at each moment of its existence as would be required to create it from scratch (if it does not yet exist). Thus, reason shows that preservation and creation differ only in the ways we think of them [and not in reality].

So I need to ask whether I have the power to cause myself (who am in existence now) to continue to exist later on. Since I am nothing but a thing that thinks . . . , if I had such a power, I would certainly be aware of it. But I can find no such power [in me]. Therefore, it is clear that my continued existence depends on something other than myself.

But maybe this being isn't God. Maybe I am the creation of my parents or of something less perfect than God. But no, there must be at least as much reality in a cause as there is in its effect (as I said before). Since I am a thinking thing with the idea of God in my mind, the cause of my existence (whatever it may be) must be a thinking thing having in it the idea of God and all His perfections. We can then go on and ask whether this thing gets its existence from itself or from something else. If it gets its existence from itself, then, obviously, it must be God -- for it would have the power to exist on its own and thus the actual power to give itself all the perfections it could think of, including all the perfections I assign to God.

However, if the cause of my existence is itself caused to exist by something else, then we will have to ask again about this other thing whether it exists from itself or from something else, until finally we will arrive at the original [first] cause, which will be God. For it is obvious that there cannot be an infinite regression of causes here, especially since I am inquiring, not only about the cause that originally produced me, but about the cause that is keeping me in existence at the present moment.

Here's a counter-argument that doesn't hold water: Maybe my existence is the result of several partial causes, and maybe I get the idea of one perfection from one cause and the idea of a second perfection

109

from a second cause and so on, so that all of the perfections I attribute to God are found somewhere in the universe, but there is, in fact, no God in whom all the perfections are combined. This doesn't work because one of God's chief perfections (according to my idea of God) is the unity, simplicity, or inseparability of all the things that are in the divine nature. My idea of the unity of all the divine perfections could have been caused only by something that gave me my ideas of all the other perfections -- for nothing could give me the idea of the inseparability of God's perfections without revealing to me what those perfections are.

Finally, as for my parents . . . , it is obvious that they are not now keeping me in existence. And insofar as I am a thinking thing, they did not even contribute to my creation. They simply formed the material [that is, the body] in which I once thought I (that is, my mind, which is what I now mean by *myself*) was contained . . . .

Conclusion of the third meditation

I am forced to this conclusion: From the simple fact that I exist and that I have in my mind the idea of a supremely perfect being, that is, God, it necessarily follows that God exists . . . . The whole argument rests on my realization that it would be impossible for me to exist as I do -- namely, with the idea of God in my mind -- if God didn't exist. It also follows that [since God is perfect] God cannot be a deceiver [because fraud and deception are caused by defects] . . . .

Meditation IV: On the Problem of Error[1]

[If God is no deceiver, how is human error with respect to truth and falsity possible, and how is that error to be explained?

Human nature is equipped with an intellect (a power of knowing) and a free will (a power of choosing), which interact in the pursuit of truth. The intellect is capable of forming beliefs that can't be doubted and therefore are certainly true. However, the intellect can also consider claims that can be doubted and that therefore may be false. The human will is free to affirm or deny propositions proposed to it by the intellect. Error results when the will (1) denies the truth, (2) affirms claims that are false, or (3) asserts knowledge where there is doubt.

Error is avoidable where a person limits his affirmations and denials to "those matters that are clearly and distinctly [indubitably] shown to . . . [the will] by the intellect . . . " and remains (more or less) neutral with respect to all claims that are subject to doubt.

Why does God permit human error? If human nature were created both free and incapable of error, it would be more perfect than it now is; but it may be that the apparent imperfection of human nature in this respect is necessary to "a greater perfection of the universe as a whole."]

---

[1]The fourth meditation is not included in this translation. Instead, a brief summary by the translator is set forth.

111

Meditation V: On Material Objects and the Existence of God

Now . . . I want to work my way out of the doubts that I raised in the first meditation and to see whether or not I can find any certainty about [the nature and existence] of material objects.

Before asking whether any such material things exist outside me, I should consider my ideas of these things and see which ones are clear and which are confused . . . .

Mathematical ideas and physical objects

[At this point, Descartes repeats what he said in the third meditation: that what he *knows* clearly and distinctly about physical objects is that they have extension (length, breadth, and depth), size, shape, location, motion, and duration. These are the aspects of material things that can be understood through mathematics, what many philosophers have called "primary qualities."]

What needs to be examined very closely here is the fact that I find within me countless ideas of things. While these things may not exist [objectively] outside of my mind, I can't say that they are nothing. Perhaps I can choose to consider these ideas or not, but I do not make up the things presented in the ideas; these things seem to have their own true and unchanging natures. For example, when I think of a triangle, it seems to me that its nature, essence, or form is completely fixed, unchanging, and eternal -- even though there may be no triangles outside of my mind. It doesn't seem that I invented the triangle, nor does it seem that its nature depends on my mind. This is obvious from the fact that I can prove many things about a triangle, for example, that its three angles are equal to two right angles and that its longest side is opposite its largest angle . . . . Whether I want to or not, I must admit the truth of these propositions, although I hadn't thought of them at all when I first thought of the triangle. This shows that I didn't just dream them up.

Some might object that perhaps the idea of a triangle came into my mind from my perceptions of triangle-shaped physical objects, that is, from external things that I have experienced through my senses. This objection is irrelevant here. I can think of many other geometrical figures that could not possibly have gotten into my mind through my senses,[1] and yet various mathematical facts about these figures can also be demonstrated (just as in the case of the triangle). Such mathematical facts are obviously true because they are clearly [and distinctly] known to me; and thus they are something rather than nothing since it is self-evident that anything that is true must be something. I have already shown that what I know clearly [and distinctly] must be true. Even if I had not proved this, still, the nature of my mind would make it impossible for me to reject what I understand clearly and distinctly. Even before I began these [skeptical] meditations, when I was absolutely convinced that the objects of sensation existed, I considered mathematical statements about figures and numbers (that is, the truths of arithmetic, geometry, and pure mathematics) to be more certain than any others.

The existence of God -- the third argument[2]

Now, if something I can think of must, in fact, have the characteristics that I clearly and distinctly think it has, can't I derive

---

[1] For example, chiliagons and myriagons, that is, thousand- and ten-thousand-sided figures.

[2] This is Descartes' version of the so-called "ontological" argument for the existence of God.

from this another proof of God's existence? I find the idea of God (a supremely perfect being) in my mind no less clearly than I find the ideas of geometrical figures and numbers. And I understand clearly and distinctly that necessary and eternal existence belongs to the divine nature just as whatever has been proved about a geometrical figure or a number belongs to the nature of the figure or number. Therefore, even if my speculations in the earlier meditations are not true, I ought to be at least as certain of God's existence as I used to be about the truths of pure mathematics.

Now, this may not be obvious at first and may even appear false. Since in all other cases I can see a difference between the existence and the essence of a thing, it seems easy to persuade myself that I can also see a difference between the existence and essence of God, so that I can think of God as nonexistent. But when I concentrate on this matter, I see clearly that God's existence can no more be separated from His essence than the essence of a triangle can be separated from the fact that its three internal angles are equal to two right angles or than the idea of a valley can be separated from the idea of a mountain. It is just as impossible to think of God (a supremely perfect being) lacking existence as it is to think of a mountain without a valley.

But from the fact that I can't *think* of God as not existing any more than I could imagine a mountain without a valley, does it necessarily follow that a mountain actually exists? From the fact that I [must] *think* of God as existing, does it follow that He actually exists? After all, thinking that something is so doesn't necessarily make it so. I can imagine a winged horse without there actually being a horse with wings. So why can't I think of God as existing even though He doesn't exist in reality?

But there is something wrong here. The fact that I can't think of a mountain without a valley doesn't require that a mountain or a valley actually exists; but it does follow that, whether they exist or not, the two

114

cannot be separated from one another. And from the fact that I cannot think of God not existing, it follows that existence cannot be separated from God and thus that He actually exists. This is not because of what I think or because my thought makes anything necessarily so, but rather because the *necessity* of the existence of God requires me to think about Him the way I do. I am simply not free to think of God without existence (that is, of a supremely perfect being without a supreme perfection), as I am free to imagine a horse with or without wings.

Someone might say that, if I claim that God has all perfections, and then claim that existence is a perfection, and then on those premises conclude that God exists, the conclusion could be avoided by denying that God has all perfections . . . . Now, I agree that it is not necessary for the idea of God to come up in my mind. However, whenever I think of the primary and supreme being and thereby bring the idea of God out of the storehouse of my mind, it *is* necessary that I assign all perfections to Him, even if I do not number all of them or list them one by one. And this, in turn, makes it necessary for me to conclude that God [the being with all perfections] exists once I see that existence is a perfection . . . .

Further, I see in many ways that the idea of God is not a creation of my mind, but a representation of a true and unchanging nature. First, God is the only being I can think of whose existence is necessarily part of its essence. Also, I cannot conceive of two or more Gods like this one; and if we assume that one such God exists, then I clearly see that He must have existed from all eternity and will exist to all eternity. Finally, I also recognize an infinity of other things in God, none of which I can either decrease or alter.

But . . . whatever argument I use, I always return to the fact that I am completely convinced only by those ideas that are clear and distinct . . . . When my mind is not overwhelmed by prejudices, and when my thoughts are not bombarded by images of perceptible things, I realize that there is nothing I know earlier or easier than facts about God. There is nothing more clear and self-evident than the existence of a supremely perfect being (that is, God), for it is to His essence alone that necessary and eternal existence belongs . . . .

God and certainty

I am now as certain of God's existence as I am of anything else that seems most certain. Beyond that, I realize that the certainty of everything else is so dependent on the existence of God that, if God did not exist, I could never know anything for certain.

My nature is such that, if I see something very clearly and distinctly, I cannot help believing it to be true. But I am also by nature incapable of permanently focusing my attention on a single thing so as to always grasp it clearly; and memories of earlier judgments often come to me when I am no longer concentrating on the reasons for those judgments. At times like that (and were I ignorant of the existence of God), someone might present an argument that would easily make me change my mind. Thus, I would never have any true and certain knowledge, but only vague and changeable opinions. For example, when I think of a triangle, it seems clear to me (steeped as I am in the principles of geometry) that the three internal angles of the triangle are equal to two right angles. I believe this to be true as long as I concentrate on its [mathematical] proof. But when I am no longer concentrating on the proof, although I may recall once grasping it clearly, I might come to doubt its truth if I were ignorant of the existence of God. For [as I pointed out in the first meditation] I can convince myself that I am so constituted by nature that I could sometimes be deceived about those things that seem most clear to me, especially when I remember that I have often believed things to be true and certain and then later on have found reasons to think them false.

116

But I now know that God exists, and that all things depend on Him, and that He is no deceiver. From this, it necessarily follows that everything I clearly and distinctly grasp is true. Even if I no longer concentrate on the reasons that led me to the knowledge of God's existence, as long as I recall that I did once clearly and distinctly know Him to exist, no counter-argument can lead me to doubt it. For now, I have true and certain knowledge of God's existence; and I am certain, not just of this, but also about everything else I can recall having once proven (such as the theorems of geometry and so on).

On what basis can these things [the things I have already proven] now be doubted? (1) That it is my nature to be always or often deceived? But I now know that I can't be wrong about what I clearly understand. (2) That much of what I took to be true and certain at one time I later realized to be false? But I didn't grasp any of that clearly and distinctly. I was ignorant of the correct standard of truth [that to be certain of anything, I must grasp it clearly and distinctly], and therefore I based my beliefs on foundations that I later found to be insecure. (3) What else then? Am I dreaming (as I myself suggested in the first meditation), so that the things I am now experiencing may be just as unreal as those that appear to me in my sleep? That does not alter the situation for, even if I *am* dreaming, anything that is evident [clear and distinct?] to my intellect is absolutely true.

I now see very clearly [and distinctly] that the knowledge of the true God is the foundation of the certainty and truth of all other knowledge. Therefore, before I was certain of God's existence, I could not be certain of anything else. But now it is possible for me to know certainly and completely an infinity of things, not only about God and other minds, but also about the material world (to the extent that it is the

117

object of pure mathematics [Latin, *quae est purae Matheseos objectum*][1]) . . . .

Meditation VI: On the Existence of the External World and Other Matters[2]

Since God is not a deceiver . . . , [He does not cause me to believe in the existence of material objects and an external world that are not really, that is, objectively, there]. He has also given me a strong (almost irresistible) natural inclination to believe that my ideas of physical objects come from those objects. If such ideas are sent to me by anything other than [actually existing] physical objects [for example, directly from God Himself], then we cannot avoid the conclusion that God is a deceiver [which is inconsistent with all our prior reasonings]. Since we know that God is *not* a deceiver, it follows that physical objects really do exist [externally and objectively]. They may not be exactly what I perceive them to be through my senses, for sense experience is unclear and confused in many ways. But physical objects must have in them at least what I clearly and distinctly conceive them to possess, namely, the properties ["primary qualities"] discerned by pure mathematics [extension, number, shape, position, etc.].

---

[1]The French reads, "*en tant qu'elle peut servir d'objet aux démonstrations des Géomètres*," that is, "in so far as it [the material world] is the object of the demonstrations of geometry."

[2]Only a small portion of the sixth mediation is included in this translation, namely, the part in which Descartes tries to show that the existence of God guarantees the truth of my belief in the existence of the world outside my mind.

118

But what about particular issues, such as the size and shape of the sun? And what about those aspects of physical objects that I grasp less clearly and distinctly than I do the mathematical ["primary"] qualities -- that is, ["secondary qualities"] such as light, sound, and pain? These, we must admit, are open to doubt. However, since God is not a deceiver, and since He has given me the ability to correct my false beliefs, I am very hopeful about finding the truth about even these kinds of things . . . .

[Therefore,] I should no longer fear that all of the things presented to me day by day through my senses are false. Rather, I should reject the exaggerated doubts raised in these meditations as ridiculous . . . . I should not have the slightest doubt as to the reality of physical objects so long as I examine them carefully with the assistance of my senses, my memory, and my mind and find no conflict between these powers. For, from the fact that God is not a deceiver, it follows that I am not deceived in any situation of this type . . . .

DAVID HUME
(1711-1776 AD)

from

AN INQUIRY CONCERNING HUMAN UNDERSTANDING[1]

Sensation and the Origin of Ideas[2]

Ideas and impressions

Everyone will quickly agree that there is a big difference between (1) a *perception* (for example, [feeling] the pain of excessive heat or the pleasure of moderate warmth), (2) the later *memory* of a perception, and (3) *imagining* a perception before one actually has it. These mental powers [memory and imagination] may mimic or copy the perceptions of the senses, but they never have the same force or vitality as a perception itself. The most we can say of them [memories and mental images], even when they are most powerful, is that they represent their object so strongly that we could almost feel or see it; but (unless a person is insane) they can never arrive at such a degree of strength that

---

[1]Paraphrased and edited by George Cronk. © 1996. For a standard edition of Hume's *Inquiry*, see *An Enquiry Concerning Human Understanding and A Letter from a Gentleman to His Friend in Edinburgh*, ed. Eric Steinberg (Indianapolis: Hackett Publishing Company, 1977).

[2]*Inquiry*, Section II.

we could not distinguish between them and actual perceptions. All the images of poetry, no matter how splendid they may be, can never describe natural objects in such a way as to make the description be taken for a real landscape. The most vivid thought is still inferior to the dullest sensation.

There is a similar difference with regard to all the other perceptions of the mind. A man in a fit of anger is aroused in a very different way from one who only thinks of that emotion. If you tell me that a person is in love, I easily understand your meaning and form a fairly accurate idea of what he feels, but I can never mistake that idea for the actual turmoil and excitement of the passion [of love]. When we reflect on our past sentiments and feelings, our thought faithfully copies its objects, but the images it employs are faint and dull compared to the images that appeared in our original perceptions. It requires no special insight or metaphysical aptitude to mark the distinction between them.

Here, therefore, we may divide all the perceptions of the mind into two classes or types, which are distinguished by their different degrees of force and liveliness. (1) The less forceful and lively are commonly called "thoughts" or "ideas." (2) There is no definite name in our language for our more forceful perceptions . . . , so let's use a little freedom and call them "impressions" . . . , by which I mean all our more lively perceptions when we [actually] hear, or see, or feel, or love, or hate, or desire, or will . . . . [I]mpressions, then, are different from ideas, which are the less lively perceptions we are aware of when we reflect on any of our impressions.

Ideas are derived from impressions

Nothing, at first glance, may seem more unlimited than human thought, which not only escapes [the control of] all human power and authority, but is not even restricted by the limits of nature and reality. To form monsters, incongruous shapes, and appearances [in the mind]

122

costs the imagination no more trouble than to think of the most natural and familiar objects. And while the body is confined to one planet, along which it creeps with pain and difficulty, thought can instantaneously take us into the most distant regions of the universe, or even beyond the universe into the limitless chaos where nature drifts into total confusion. Although something has never been seen or heard of, it can be imagined by the mind. Nothing is beyond the power of thought except . . . an absolute contradiction [for example, we cannot think that a square has more or less than four sides].

But while our thought seems to have this unrestricted liberty, we shall find when we look more closely that it is really confined within very narrow limits. All this creative power of the mind amounts to no more than the ability to take the materials presented to us by the senses and put them together, change them, add to them, or subtract from them in various ways. When we think of a golden mountain, we merely join two already familiar ideas that are consistent with one another, that is, "gold" and "mountain." We can conceive of a virtuous horse because . . . we can think of virtue, and this we can unite with the figure and shape of a horse, which is an animal already familiar to us. In short, all the materials of thinking are derived either from our outward or from our inward sensations. The mind and the will are able to mix and compose these materials in various ways. To express myself in philosophical language, all of our ideas (that is, our more feeble perceptions) are copies of our impressions (that is, our more vivid perceptions).

This can be proved by way of two arguments. *First*, when we analyze our thoughts and ideas, however intricate and sublime they may be, we always find that they can be reduced to certain simple ideas that have been copied from an earlier feeling or sensation [that is, an impression]. Even those ideas that at first seem farthest from sense experience are found, when examined closely, to be derived from it. The idea of God -- that is, the idea of an infinitely intelligent, wise, and good being -- arises from our reflecting on the processes of our own minds and extending our own qualities of goodness and wisdom to infinity. We may push this kind of investigation as far as we wish, but we shall always find that every idea we examine is copied from an impression that is similar to the idea. Those who claim that this is not universally true nor without exception will have to present an idea that, in their opinion, is not derived from sensation. Then, if we are to maintain our theory, we will have to produce the impression or lively perception that corresponds to the idea.

Secondly, if we find a person who is incapable of a certain kind of sensation (because of some defect in the relevant sense organ), we also find that he is incapable of forming the corresponding idea. A blind person has no notion of colors, and a deaf person has no idea of sounds. Restore sight to the blind person or hearing to the deaf person . . . , and then neither of them will have any difficulty in forming ideas of colors or sounds because an inlet for sensations is also an inlet for ideas. It is the same where an object that can excite a sensation has never been encountered by the relevant sense organ. A Laplander or Negro [African?] has no idea of how enjoyable wine is. And there may be people who have never felt, or who are completely incapable of having, certain sentiments or passions that are common to the human race . . . . For example, a mild-mannered person can form no idea of deep-rooted revenge and cruelty, nor can a selfish heart easily imagine the heights of friendship and generosity. It seems quite possible that other beings may possess many senses of which we can have no conception because the ideas of them have never been introduced to us in the only way in which an idea can enter the mind, that is, by the actual feeling and sensation.

A possible exception

There is, however, one . . . phenomenon that may show that it is not *absolutely* impossible for ideas to arise independently of their

124

corresponding [sense] impressions. I think we all agree that the several distinct ideas of color, which enter by the eye, or those of sound, which are conveyed by the ear, are really different from each other, although at the same time they resemble one another. Now, if that's true of different colors, it must be no less true of the different *shades* of the same color. Each shade produces a distinct idea, independent of the rest. If this were not the case, then it would be possible (by the continual gradation of shades) to run a color . . . into what is most remote from it; and if you will not allow any of the intermediate shades to be different, you cannot, without absurdity, deny that the extremes are the same.

Imagine, then, a person who has enjoyed his sight for thirty years and who has become perfectly familiar with colors of all kinds except for one particular shade of blue . . . , which he has never seen. Now let all the different shades of that color [blue], except for that single one, be placed before him, descending gradually from the deepest to the lightest. It is obvious that he will perceive a blank where that shade is missing, and he will sense that there is a greater distance in that place between the neighboring colors than in any other. Isn't it possible for him, from his own imagination, to supply what is missing and to construct for himself the idea of that particular shade, even though it has never been presented to him by his senses? I think almost everyone will agree that he can do so; and this may serve as a proof that the simple ideas [in the mind] are not always, in every instance, derived from the corresponding [sense] impressions. However, this case is so unusual that it is hardly worth mentioning, and it is not so important that we should change our general theory because of it.

Testing ideas on the basis of sense impressions

Here, therefore, is a proposition that not only seems simple and understandable in itself, but, if it were used properly, it might make every [philosophical] debate equally understandable and get rid of all the gobbledygook that has for so long infected metaphysical investigations and drawn disgrace upon them. [On the one hand,] all *ideas*, especially abstract ones, are naturally faint and unclear. The mind has only a slight grasp of them, and they are likely to be confused with other similar ideas. Also, when we have used a term a lot, but without giving it a really exact meaning, we are likely to imagine [mistakenly] that it has a definite idea connected to it . . . . [On the other hand,] all *impressions* -- that is, all sensations either outward or inward -- are strong and vivid. The lines between them are more exactly determined, and it is not easy to fall into any error or mistake with regard to them.

Therefore, when we have any suspicion that a philosophical term is employed without any real meaning or [specific] idea [attached to it] (as is done very frequently), we need only inquire, *"From what impression is that alleged idea derived?"* And if it is impossible to identify any [such sense impression], this will serve to confirm our suspicion [that the idea or term in question has no foundation in reality]. By bringing ideas into so clear a light, we may reasonably hope to remove all disputes that may arise concerning their nature and reality . . . .

The Nature and Limits of Human Knowledge[1]

Relations of ideas and matters of fact

All the objects of human reason or inquiry may naturally be divided into two kinds: *relations of ideas* and *matters of fact*. Relations

---

[1] *Inquiry*, Section IV, Part I.

of ideas are studied by the sciences of geometry, algebra, and arithmetic. In fact, any claim that is either intuitively or demonstrably certain has to do with relations of ideas. *That the square of the hypotenuse is equal to [the sum of] the square[s] of the [other] two sides [of a right triangle]*[1] is a proposition that expresses a relation between these figures. *That three times five is equal to one half of thirty* expresses a relation between these numbers. Propositions of this kind are discoverable by thought alone, regardless of what actually exists in the universe. Even if there were no circles or triangles in nature, the [geometrical] truths demonstrated by Euclid[2] would be certain and evident.

---

[1]This is a geometrical truth known traditionally as "the Pythagorean theorem." A right angle is an angle of 90°, formed by the meeting of two straight lines that are perpendicular to each other. A right (or right-angled) triangle is a triangle containing one right angle. In such a triangle, the square of the side opposite to the right angle (the "hypotenuse") is equal to the sum of the squares of the other two sides adjoining the right angle. For example, a triangle whose sides are three, four, and five feet long, respectively, has a right angle formed by the sides that are three and four feet long, respectively, and the side that is five feet long is the hypotenuse.

In accordance with the theorem, $3^2 + 4^2 = 5^2$, that is, $9 + 16 = 25$.

[2]Euclid (fl. c. 300 BC) is the author of the classic, *Elements [of Geometry]*.

Matters of fact . . . are not established in the same manner [as relations of ideas]. Furthermore, no matter how strong the evidence is for some matter of fact, it is not of the same nature as the evidence for the truth of a judgment concerning relations of ideas. Every judgment concerning matters of fact can be denied without contradiction; and the opposite of any such judgment can be thought of by the mind quite easily and distinctly . . . . *That the sun will not rise tomorrow* is a statement that is just as comprehensible and no more contradictory than the claim *that it will rise*. We cannot show that the claim that the sun will not rise tomorrow is *necessarily* false. If we *could* prove that claim to be necessarily false, it would be a contradiction, and then it could never be clearly conceived of by the mind.

What is the foundation of factual knowledge?

It may therefore be worthwhile to inquire into the nature of the evidence that assures us of the real existence of any matter of fact. Is there any such evidence of matters of fact other than the present witness of our senses or the records of our memory? This issue has not been much explored in the history of philosophy, so we may be excused for any doubts and errors that may arise as we pursue this investigation. After all, we will be marching along very difficult paths without any guidance or direction [from philosophers of the past]. Our doubts and errors may even prove useful by stimulating curiosity and also by undermining the overly confident faith and security [of common sense], which is . . . [such an obstacle to] all reasoning and free inquiry. I assume that it will not be a discouragement if we discover defects in the common philosophy, but rather an incentive to develop a philosophy that is more complete and satisfactory than what has so far been proposed to the public.

All thinking about matters of fact seems to be based on the relation of *cause and effect*. Only by means of that relation can we go

128

beyond the evidence of our memory and senses. If you were to ask someone why he believes any matter of fact that is not present to him (for example, that his friend is in the country or in France), he would give you a reason, and this reason would be some other fact (for example, a letter received from his friend, or his knowledge of his friend's previous decisions and promises). If someone were to find a watch or any other machine on a desert island, he would conclude that there had once been human beings on that island. All our reasonings about [matters of] fact are of the same nature. And here it is constantly assumed that there is a connection between the present fact and that which is inferred from it. Were there nothing to bind them together, the inference would be entirely groundless. The hearing of an articulate voice and rational discussion in the dark assures us of the presence of some person. Why? Because these are . . . effects closely associated with the makeup of a human being. If we analyze all reasonings of this nature [that is, concerning matters of fact], we shall find that they are founded on the relation of cause and effect . . . . Heat and light are . . . effects of fire, and the one effect may be legitimately inferred from the other.

Therefore, if we want to know the nature of the evidence that assures us of matters of fact, we must find out how we arrive at the knowledge of cause and effect.

Knowledge of cause and effect arises entirely from experience

I propose the following general proposition, which admits of no exception: the knowledge of the relation between cause and effect is not in any sense arrived at through *a priori* reasoning [that is, reasoning prior to or independently of experience]; on the contrary, such knowledge arises entirely from experience [*a posteriori*], namely, the experience of finding that any two things are constantly conjoined with each other.

Imagine that an object is presented to a person with very strong reasoning and intellectual ability. If that object is entirely new to him, he will not be able to discover any of its causes or effects, no matter how closely he examines its perceptible qualities. Adam, even if his reasoning ability was initially perfect, could not have inferred from the fluidity and transparency of water that it could drown him, nor could he have inferred from the light and warmth of fire that it could burn him up. No object reveals through the qualities that appear to the senses either the causes that produced it or the effects that will arise from it; nor can human reason, without assistance from experience, infer anything about what really exists or about matters of fact in general.

This proposition, that causes and effects are discoverable, not by reason, but by experience, must be accepted with regard to objects that were once completely unknown to us, since we recall that we were then utterly unable to predict what would arise from them. If you show two smooth pieces of marble to someone with no scientific knowledge, he will never discover that they will hold together so strongly that it would take a very great force to separate them in a direct line, while they are easily separated by lateral pressure. Such phenomena that do not follow the expected course of nature are obviously knowable only by way of experience. No one can imagine that the explosion of gunpowder or the attraction of a lodestone could ever be discovered by *a priori* arguments. Similarly, when an effect depends on intricate machinery or secret structure of parts, we . . . attribute all our knowledge of it to experience. Who will claim that he can give the ultimate reason why milk or bread is proper nourishment for human beings but not for lions or tigers?

But what about events that have been familiar to us from our infancy, that seem to follow the expected course of nature, and that seem to be based on the simple qualities of objects and not on any secret structure of parts? We might think that we could discover these effects

130

through reason alone, without experience. We might fancy that, if we were brought suddenly into this world, we could have immediately inferred that one billiard ball would communicate motion to another on impact, and that we could have been certain of this without waiting for the event to actually occur. Such is the influence of custom. Where it is strongest, it not only covers our natural ignorance, but it even conceals itself and seems not to be there merely because . . . [we are so used to it].

Perhaps the following reflections will be sufficient to convince us that all the laws of nature and absolutely all the operations of physical things are knowable only through experience. Suppose an object were presented to us and we were required to describe its effects without consulting past observations. How would we proceed? We would have to invent or imagine what such effects might be; and it is obvious that this invention will be completely arbitrary. No matter how hard we think and reason about the object, we could never find its effects that way. For an effect is totally different from its cause and thus can never be discovered in it. Motion in the second billiard ball is quite distinct from motion in the first; nor is there anything in the one to suggest the smallest hint of the other. A stone or piece of metal raised into the air and left without any support immediately falls. But to consider the matter without reference to experience, would there be any *reason* to insist that the stone or metal *must* fall downward rather than upward or in any other direction?

Thus, the assumption that there is a tie or connection between a cause and its effect that makes it impossible for any other effect to follow from that cause is also arbitrary. For example, when I see a billiard ball moving in a straight line toward another, and even if I happened to believe that motion in the second ball would result from the contact . . . between the two balls, can't I think that a hundred different events might as well follow from that cause? May not both balls remain at absolute rest? May not the first ball return in a straight line [to where

131

it started], or leap off from the second in any line or direction? None of these suppositions is logically contradictory, and thus each of them is conceivable. Why then should we give the preference to one that is no more consistent or conceivable than the rest? None of our reasonings *a priori* will ever be able to provide any foundation for this preference.

In a word, then, every effect is a distinct event from its cause. Therefore, it could not be discovered in the cause, and any *a priori* idea that a given cause will result in a given effect must be entirely arbitrary. Even after a particular effect is suggested, its conjunction with the cause must appear equally arbitrary since there are always many other effects that, as far as we can tell from reason alone, might just as consistently and naturally follow from the cause. Therefore, any attempt to predict any single event or to infer any particular effect from a cause on the basis of reason alone, without the assistance of observation and experience, cannot succeed.

This is why no philosopher or scientist who is rational and modest has ever pretended to discover the ultimate cause of any natural operation or to reveal the action of any power that produces any single effect in the universe. All that human reason can hope to accomplish is to reduce the principles that govern natural phenomena to a greater simplicity and to trace the many particular effects [in the world] to a few general causes -- all on the basis of analogy, experience, and observation. But we would be wasting our time if we tried to discover the [ultimate] causes of these general causes. No particular explanation of them will ever satisfy us. These ultimate springs and principles [that is, the ultimate causes of things] are totally shut off from human curiosity and inquiry . . . .

The Nature and Limits of Inductive Reasoning

The problem of induction[1]

When it is asked, *What is the nature of all our reasonings concerning matters of fact?*, the proper answer seems to be that they are based on the relation of cause and effect. And when it is asked, *What is the basis of all our reasonings and conclusions concerning the relation of cause and effect?*, it may be replied in one word, EXPERIENCE. And if we go further and ask, *What is the foundation of all conclusions from experience?*, this raises a new question that may be harder to answer . . . .

It will certainly be agreed that nature has kept us at a great distance from all her secrets and has given us only the knowledge of a few surface qualities of objects, while she conceals from us those powers and principles that cause these objects to be what they are and to do what they do. Our senses show us the color, weight, and texture of bread; but neither sensation nor reasoning can show us those qualities that make the bread nourishing to the human body. Sight or feeling gives us an idea of the actual motion of physical objects; but we are unable to form even a vague conception of the wonderful force or power that would carry a moving object on forever through space unless it were to come into contact with other bodies and convey the power to them.

But in spite of our ignorance of natural powers and principles, we always presume that [different] objects with the same perceptible qualities have the same secret powers and will produce effects similar to those we have experienced [in the past]. If we observe something with

---

[1]*Inquiry*, Section IV, Part II.

133

the same color and texture of the bread that we have eaten in the past, we do not hesitate to eat it, and we are certain that it will provide us with the same nourishment and support. This is the process of thinking that I am now interested in. What is its foundation . . . ? Why should our past experience of objects and their effects be extended into the future and to other objects that for all we know may be similar only in appearance? This is my main question at this point.

The bread that I ate in the past nourished me; that is, a physical object with certain perceptible qualities had, at that time, the power to nourish me. But does it follow *necessarily* that some other bread will also be nourishing to me at another [future] time and that the same perceptible qualities will always have the same secret powers? This doesn't seem necessary to me. Surely, that the mind is drawing these conclusions [from past experience], that it is taking a certain step, following a process of thought, making an inference -- all this needs to be explained.

The following propositions do not have the same meaning: (1) *I have found that such an object has always been accompanied by such an effect* and (2) *I foresee that other objects that appear similar to the former object will be accompanied by similar effects.* I will agree for the sake of argument that the second proposition may legitimately be inferred from the first; I know in fact that it always is [so] inferred. But if you insist that the inference is made by a process of logical reasoning, then I want you to present that reasoning . . . .

[At this point, Hume argues that there is no *logical* requirement that conditions and relations discovered in past experience will continue to hold true in the future. He holds that the common belief that the order of events experienced in the future will be consistent with the order of events experienced in the past cannot by any means be proved true. This is what is known as "the problem of induction." It is called that because induction is the process of drawing inferences from past or

134

present observations to future events and situations. Hume is saying that the process of induction has no strictly logical justification. Should we agree with him?]

Of course, it is obvious that the most ignorant and stupid peasants -- and even infants and animals -- improve by experience and learn the qualities of natural objects by observing the effects that result from them. When a child has felt the sensation of pain from touching the flame of a candle, he will be careful not to put his hand near *any* candle; for he will expect a similar effect from a similar cause. If you claim that the child is led to this conclusion by any process of argument or reasoning, then I require you to produce the argument, and you shouldn't refuse such a fair demand. You can't get away with saying that the argument is too abstract for you since, after all, you believe that it is obvious to a mere infant! Therefore, if you can't present the argument, or if you present one that is intricate or profound, then you're refuting yourself. You've got to admit that it isn't logic and argumentation that leads us to believe that the past resembles the future [or vice versa] and to expect similar effects from apparently similar causes . . . .

The foundation of induction[1]

[Then what is it?] Suppose a person with the strongest powers of reasoning and reflection is brought suddenly into this world. He would immediately observe a continual succession of objects, one event following another, but he wouldn't be able to see anything else. He wouldn't be able to "reason out" the idea of cause and effect because the . . . [ultimate causes of natural events] never appear to the senses. It isn't reasonable to conclude that one event is the cause of another

---

[1] *Inquiry*, Section V.

135

simply because one occurs before the other. Their conjunction may be accidental. There may be no reason to infer the existence of one from the appearance of the other. In a word, without more experience, such a person could never . . . be sure of anything beyond what was immediately present to his memory and senses.

Suppose further that he has acquired more experience and has lived long enough in the world to have observed similar objects or events to be *constantly conjoined* together. What follows from this experience? He immediately infers the existence of one object from the appearance of the other; but he hasn't . . . gained any idea or knowledge of the secret power by which the one object produces the other, nor does logic require him to draw this inference. Nonetheless, he finds himself compelled to draw it, and he would continue to think this way even if he were himself convinced that logic has nothing to do with it. There is some other principle [that is, something other than logic] that compels him to form such a conclusion.

This principle is CUSTOM or HABIT . . . . [Repeated observations of events that are constantly conjoined with one another *accustom* or *habituate* us to believe that one event is the *cause* of another, which we believe to be the *effect* of the prior event, and to expect the future to resemble the past.] All inferences from experience, therefore, are effects of custom [and habit], not of logical reasoning.

Custom [or habit], then, is the great guide of human life. It is that principle alone that makes our experience useful to us and makes us expect that the future train of events will be similar to those that have appeared in the past. Without the influence of custom [and habit], we would be completely ignorant of every matter of fact beyond what is immediately present to the memory and senses. We would never know how to adjust means to ends or how to use our natural powers to produce any effect. There would be an end at once of all action as well as of most speculation . . . .

136

All beliefs as to matters of fact or actual existence are derived merely from some object that is present to the memory or senses and a customary [or habitual] conjunction between that and some other object. In other words, having found in many instances that any two kinds of objects (flame and heat, snow and cold, etc.) have always been conjoined together, the mind is then carried by custom [and habit] to expect either heat or cold when flame or snow is again presented to the senses . . . . The transition of thought from cause to effect does not proceed from reason. It originates entirely from custom [habit] and experience . . . .

The Idea that there is a Necessary Connection between Cause and Effect[1]

It seems beyond reasonable dispute that all our ideas are nothing but copies of our impressions, or, in other words, that it is impossible for us to *think* of anything that we have not previously *felt*, either by our external or internal senses . . . . Therefore, to fully understand the idea of . . . [the] necessary connection [between cause and effect], we must look for the [sense] impression from which it is derived.

There is no sense impression of causal power or necessary connection

[However,] when we observe external objects and consider the operation of causes, we can never, not even in a single instance, discover any [causal] power or necessary connection or any [other] quality that binds the effect to the cause so as to make the one a certain

---

[1] *Inquiry*, Section VII.

consequence of the other. We find only that the one does actually, in fact, follow the other. The motion of one billiard ball is followed by motion in the second. This is all that appears to the *outward* senses. The mind gets no sensation or *inward* impression from this succession of objects. So there isn't any basis in [external] perception for the idea of . . . necessary connection . . . . It is impossible . . . that the idea of [causal] power [or necessary connection between cause and effect] can be derived from the observation of particular instances of the operation of external objects because external objects never reveal any power that could give rise to this idea . . . .

[The same is true of internal perception.] It seems that the will can move [some of] our bodily organs and [to some extent] direct the operations of our mind. An act of will can produce motion in our limbs or raise a new idea in our imagination . . . . But we are in no way immediately conscious of the *means* by which these acts of will are effected; the *energy* by which the will performs such extraordinary operations is always beyond our most careful observations . . . . [We can experience an act of the will and the change of body or mind that follows it; but there is no perception or impression of the force, power, or energy by which the will can bring about such changes in the body or in the mind.]

The empirical source of the ideas of causal power and necessary connection

[Thus,] all events seem entirely loose and separate. One event follows another, but we can never observe any tie between them. They seem *conjoined* but never *connected* . . . . Therefore, it *seems* that we must conclude that we have no idea of [necessary] connection or [causal] power at all and that these words are absolutely without any meaning, whether they are used in philosophical discussions or in common life. But there is a way to avoid this conclusion, for there is a

138

[possible] source   [of the ideas of causal power and necessary connection] that we have not yet examined . . . .

When a particular kind of event has always, in all instances, been conjoined with another, we do not hesitate to predict one upon the appearance of the other. We then employ the only principle that can convince us of any matter of fact or [real] existence. We then call the one event *cause* and the other *effect*. We *assume* that there is some connection between them, some power in the one by which it necessarily and certainly produces the other.

It appears, then, that the idea of a necessary connection between events arises from a number of similar instances in which such events are *constantly conjoined* with one another . . . . [A]fter a repetition of [such] similar instances, the mind is carried by habit to the belief that, upon the appearance of one event, there will inevitably follow another event that usually accompanies the first. Therefore, this connection, which we *feel* in the mind, this customary movement of the imagination from one object to its usual companion -- *this* is the sensation or impression from which we form the idea of [causal] power or necessary connection [between cause and effect] . . . .

The first time someone saw the communication of motion by one billiard ball to another, he could not conclude that the one event was [causally] *connected* to the other but only that the two were *conjoined*. After he has observed several instances of this . . . *conjunction*, he then pronounces the two events to be *connected* . . . . When we say, therefore, that one object is [causally] connected with another, we mean only that they have acquired a connection in our thought, which then leads us to infer the existence [or occurrence] of one from the existence [or occurrence] of the other . . . .

We say, for instance, that the vibration of this string is the cause of this particular sound. But what do we mean by that . . . ? We either

139

mean *that this vibration is followed by this sound and that [in our past experience] all similar vibrations have been followed by similar sounds,* or [we mean] *that this vibration is followed by this sound and that, upon the appearance of one, the mind outruns the senses and forms an idea of the other [even before it has appeared].* We may consider the relation of cause and effect in either of these two ways; but beyond these, we have no idea of it.

Summary and conclusion

Now, let's summarize the argument of this section: Every idea is copied from some prior impression or sensation; and where we cannot find any impression, we may be certain that there is no idea. In all single instances of the operations of bodies or minds, there is nothing that produces any impression (and thus nothing that gives rise to any idea) of [causal] power or necessary connection [of cause and effect]. However, when there are many uniform instances in which the same object is always followed by the same event, we then begin to entertain the notion of a necessary connection between events that we come to call "cause" and "effect." We then *feel* a new sensation or impression, that is, a customary connection in thought or imagination between one object and its usual companion.

This sensation is the origin of the idea . . . [of necessary connection]. For as this idea arises from a number of similar instances and not from any single instance, it must arise from that circumstance in which many instances differ from a single individual instance. But this customary connection . . . in the imagination is the only circumstance in which they differ. In every other way they are alike. To return to an obvious illustration, the first time we saw one billiard ball move after another had moved into contact with it is exactly the same as any [such] instance that may now appear to us, except . . . that we could not, at first, *infer* one event from the other. We can now make such an inference since we have for a long time observed and experienced the same thing happening uniformly over and over again.

I don't know whether the reader will easily understand what I am trying to say. I am afraid of multiplying words about it or of presenting it in more various ways since it might then become [even] more unclear and complicated. In abstract reasoning, there is always a certain point of view that can explain the subject better than all the eloquence and abundant expression in the world. This is the point of view we should try to reach, and we should reserve the flowers of rhetoric for subjects that are more suited to them . . . .

The Value and Limitations of Skepticism[1]

What is skepticism, and how far can skeptical doubt and uncertainty be pushed? [Hume now proceeds to define, analyze, and evaluate various types of skepticism.]

Antecedent skepticism

There is a kind of skepticism that *precedes* all inquiry and philosophical speculation. [Hume calls this "antecedent skepticism."] This is recommended by Descartes and others as a way of avoiding error and hasty judgment. What they propose is total doubt, not only with regard to our beliefs and principles, but also with regard to our mental and perceptual abilities. We should, they say, accept only those beliefs that are deduced from some first principle that cannot possibly be false or misleading [a principle that is beyond all doubt]. The problem with this is, of course, that there is no such original principle

---

[1] *Inquiry*, Section XII.

141

that stands above all others that are self-evident and convincing or, if there is, we could make deductions from it only by using the very mental abilities that this kind of skepticism has cast doubt on. Thus, even if Cartesian skepticism were humanly possible (which it isn't), it would be entirely incurable. No amount of reasoning could ever bring us to a state of assurance and conviction on any subject whatever.

However, this kind of skepticism may be developed in a more moderate and reasonable way, and then it can serve as a necessary preparation for the study of philosophy. That is, it can help us achieve a proper impartiality in our judgments and can free our minds from those prejudices that we may have picked up from [a poor] education or from careless [common] opinion. To begin with clear and self-evident principles, to move ahead by cautious and sure steps, to review frequently and critically our conclusions and their implications -- although this process is time-consuming, it is the only method by which we can ever hope to reach truth and attain a proper stability and certainty in our conclusions.

Consequent skepticism

There is also another kind of skepticism that, according to some thinkers, arises *after* [or as a result of] scientific [and philosophical] inquiry. [Hume calls this "consequent skepticism."] Through scientific and philosophical investigations, it is said, we discover either the absolute unreliability of our mental powers or their inability to reach any certainty on the various subjects of human speculation. Some philosophers even dispute the trustworthiness of our senses, and they also raise as much doubt about our common sense beliefs as they do about the most profound . . . conclusions of metaphysics or theology. Since this kind of skepticism is found in [the works of] some philosophers and is refuted by several others, it arouses our curiosity and makes us inquire into the arguments on which it rests.

142

Arguments in support of consequent skepticism

I need not go into the more common criticisms by the skeptics of all ages against the evidence of the senses . . . : [for example,] the crooked appearance of an oar in water; the various ways in which objects at different distances from us appear; the double images that result from the pressing of one eye; and many other such cases. These examples, often cited by skeptics, only show that the senses are not entirely reliable and that we must use reason to correct our sense perceptions, taking into account the nature of the medium [through which we are perceiving something], the distance of the object [from us], and the nature of the sense organ [we are using] . . . .

But there are other more profound arguments against the reliability of sense perception, and these are not so easily refuted. It seems obvious that people naturally tend to trust their senses. On this basis, and without depending on reason or argumentation, we assume the existence of an external universe; and we believe that the existence of this universe does not depend on our perceptions but would exist even if we and all other sentient creatures were absent or destroyed. Even [non-human] animals -- in all their thoughts, plans, and actions -- [seem to] hold this belief in the objective existence of external objects.

(1) Common sense realism

It also seems obvious . . . that people take their mental images of external objects -- the images being derived from sense impressions -- to *be* those objects. Most people never suspect that these images are nothing but *representations* of external objects. This table -- which we see to be white and which is hard to the touch -- is believed to exist independently of our perceptions and to be something external to the mind that perceives it. Our presence does not make it exist; our absence does not cause its nonexistence. Its existence is uniformly and entirely independent of the intelligent beings who perceive or think about it.

143

But these common sense beliefs about external objects are easily undermined by a little philosophical reflection. Nothing can be present to the mind but an image or perception. The senses are only the inlets through which these images are conveyed to the mind. There is no direct contact between the mind and the [external] object. The table we see seems to get smaller as we move away from it; but the real table, which exists independently of us, does not actually get smaller. Our idea of the table is nothing but a mental image [and the image, which is present to the mind, is not the table itself]. These are the obvious dictates of reason, and no reflective person has ever doubted that the things that we call "this house" and "that tree" are nothing but perceptions in the mind, fleeting copies or representations of the things themselves, which are what they are, independently of our perceptions and thoughts.

(2) Representationalism

Reason, therefore, requires us to depart from common sense beliefs and to embrace a new point of view with regard to the evidence of the senses. But here philosophy finds herself extremely embarrassed when she tries to justify this new point of view and to defeat the quibbles and objections of the skeptics. She cannot appeal to [so-called] infallible and irresistible natural instincts since "natural" beliefs [about the external world] have been shown to be fallible or even erroneous. Nor is it humanly possible to prove this new philosophical point of view through clear and convincing argumentation.

By what argument can it be proved that the perceptions of the mind must be caused by external objects, which are completely different from those perceptions but which resemble them (if that be possible)? How can it be proved that such perceptions could not arise either from the energy of the mind itself, or from the suggestions of some invisible and unknown spirit, or from some other cause still more unknown to us? We know, in fact, that many mental images arise in dreams or through madness and other diseases and are not perceptions of anything external to the mind. Furthermore, nothing can be more inexplicable than how a material object can convey an image of itself to the mind since mind and matter are substances with very different or even contrary natures.

Whether sense perceptions are caused by external objects that resemble them is a question of fact. How can this question be answered? Only by experience. All questions of fact must be answered by experience. But in this case experience is and must be entirely silent. The mind never has anything present to it but perceptions. The mind cannot possibly have any experience of the connection of its perceptions with [external] objects. Therefore, the assumption that there is such a connection is without any foundation in . . . [experience].

(3) God and the reliability of sense perception

To try to prove the reliability of the senses on the basis of the reliability of the Supreme Being [God] is surely making a very unexpected circuit. If God's truthfulness were at all relevant to this matter, our senses would be completely infallible, since it is impossible for God to ever deceive. Not to mention that, once we call the existence of the external world into question, we are then at a loss to find arguments by which we may prove the existence of God or any of his attributes.

(4) Skeptical conclusion

On this subject, then, the more profound and philosophical skeptics will always win when they seek to raise doubts about all human knowledge . . . . If you try to defend the reliability of sense experience on the basis of natural instinct and inclination, then you will believe that the mental image [of an external object] *is* the object. If you disclaim this "natural" and "common sense" conclusion in favor of the more rational opinion that mental images are only representations of external objects . . . , then you will never find any convincing argument from experience to prove that there is any connection between perceptions and external objects . . . .

[Thus, the belief that sense perception reveals the existence and nature of the external world cannot be proved.] If we base that belief on natural instinct, it leads to conclusions that are contrary to reason; and if we base the belief on reason, we then act contrary to natural instinct and at the same time can find no convincing evidence of any connection between perception and the external world . . . . Also, if we accept the view that all sensible qualities [of external objects] are [impressions] in the mind rather than in the objects, then we are left with only a certain unknown, inexplicable *something* as the cause of our perceptions, a notion so general and vague that no skeptic will think it worthwhile to argue against it . . . .

Skepticism concerning mathematical reasoning

The chief skeptical objection to abstract [mathematical?] reasoning is derived from the ideas of space and time.[1] In everyday life

---

[1] In this part of the *Inquiry*, Section XII, Part II (second, third, and fourth paragraphs), Hume presents three examples of "absurdities and contradictions" that follow logically from the mathematical idea of the infinite divisibility of space and time. However, he does not explain exactly *why* these examples are absurd or contradictory. Hume proposes a solution to these problems based upon a denial that space and time are infinitely divisible. See footnote 66 on page 109 in *An Enquiry Concerning Human Understanding and A Letter from a Gentleman to His Friend in Edinburgh*, ed. Eric Steinberg (Indianapolis: Hackett Publishing Company, 1977), as well as Hume's more comprehensive discussion of these issues in Book I,

and from a superficial point of view, these ideas seem very clear and intelligible. But when they are examined very closely, they turn out to be full of absurdity and contradiction. [For example,] no religious dogmas, invented in order to tame and subdue the rebellious reason of mankind, ever shocked common sense more than the implications and consequences of *the doctrine of the infinite divisibility of space* . . . .

[Imagine] *a real quantity [of space], infinitely less than another finite quantity [of space] and containing quantities [of space] infinitely less than itself, and so on to infinity.* This is such a bold and extraordinary concept that it shocks the clearest and most natural principles of human reason, and it would seem that no demonstration could possibly support this idea. But what is even more extraordinary is that [in the mathematical study of space] this seemingly absurd concept *is* supported by a chain of reasoning that is most clear and natural. We can't accept the premises without admitting the consequences.

Furthermore, nothing can be more convincing and satisfactory than all the conclusions concerning the properties of circles and triangles. And yet, once we accept these conclusions, how can we deny *(1) that the angle of contact between a circle and its tangent is infinitely less than any rectilinear angle, (2) that, as you may increase the diameter of the circle to infinity, this angle of contact becomes still less, even to infinity, and (3) that the angle of contact between other curves and their tangents may be infinitely less than those between any circle and its tangent, and so on to infinity?* The mathematical proof of these principles seems as solid as that which proves the three angles of a triangle to be equal to two right ones, although the latter principle is

---

Part II, of *A Treatise of Human Nature*, ed. Ernest C. Mossner (New York: Penguin Books, 1969).

natural and understandable, while the former is full of contradiction and absurdity.

Reason here seems to be thrown into a kind of amazement and suspense, which, without the suggestions of any skeptic, makes her uncertain of herself and of the ground on which she walks. She sees a full light that illuminates certain places; but that light borders upon the most profound darkness. And between these, she is so dazzled and perplexed that she can hardly speak with certainty and assurance about anything.

The absurdity of these bold conclusions that follow from the mathematical analysis of space seems, if possible, even more pronounced with regard to *time*. *An infinite number of real parts of time, passing in succession and exhausted one after another*, seems so evidently a contradiction that no one . . . whose judgment is not corrupted instead of being improved by the [mathematical] sciences would ever be able to accept it.

Nonetheless, reason must remain restless and troubled with regard to this skepticism [about mathematical reasoning] to which she is driven by these seeming absurdities and contradictions [about space and time]. How any clear and distinct idea can contain elements contradictory to itself or to any other clear and distinct idea is absolutely incomprehensible and is, perhaps, as absurd as any proposition that can be formed. Nothing, therefore, can be more subject to doubt and hesitation than this sort of skepticism itself, this skepticism [about abstract reasoning] that arises from some of the paradoxical conclusions of geometry or the science of quantity [arithmetic and algebra?].

Extreme skepticism concerning knowledge of matters of fact

Skeptical objections to . . . [human] reasoning concerning matters of fact fall into two categories: *popular* and *philosophical*. The

148

popular objections are based on the natural weakness of the human mind; the contradictory opinions that have been held in different times and nations; the variations between our judgments made in sickness and health, youth and old age, prosperity and adversity; the continual disputes as to each particular person's opinions and sentiments . . . ; etc. There is no need to dwell on these objections, which are very weak. In everyday life, we continually think and argue about matters of fact, and we cannot live without this kind of thought and argument. Popular skepticism will never be able to stop that process. What undermines this and all forms of extreme skepticism is action, and employment, and the occupations of everyday life.

Extreme skepticism may prosper and triumph in the schools, where it is indeed difficult, if not impossible, to refute it. But when this kind of skepticism . . . is brought into contact with everyday realities that excite our passions and sentiments, it comes into conflict with the powerful inclinations of human nature. At that point, skeptical doubts vanish like smoke, and even the most determined skeptic is then in the same condition as other people.

Therefore, the extreme skeptic had better confine himself to presenting more *philosophical* objections . . . [concerning our knowledge of matters of fact]. Here, the skeptic . . . may justly insist (1) that all evidence for any matter of fact that lies beyond the testimony of sensation or memory is derived entirely from the relation of cause and effect; (2) that the only basis of the idea of the cause and effect relationship is the fact that two objects [which we call "cause" and "effect"] have [in our past experience] been frequently conjoined together; (3) that we have no convincing proof that objects that have been frequently conjoined in our past experience will continue in the future to be conjoined in the same manner . . . ; (4) that nothing leads us to infer their future conjunction but custom [habit] or a certain instinct in our nature; and (5) that while that instinct is indeed difficult to resist, it just might be, like other instincts, fallacious and deceitful. As long as

149

the skeptic sticks to these claims, he is on solid ground in his insistence on the limitations of our factual knowledge. Here, skepticism seems, at least for the time being, to destroy all assurance and conviction.

Why we should reject extreme skepticism

We might develop these skeptical arguments further if there were any reason to expect them to be beneficial to society. But this is the major objection to excessive skepticism: no enduring good can ever result from it . . . . We need only ask such a skeptic what his meaning is and what he proposes to accomplish by all these curious arguments. He is then at a loss and doesn't know how to answer us . . . .

An extreme skeptic cannot expect his philosophy to have any lasting influence on the human mind; and if it did have such an influence, the skeptic cannot believe that this would be beneficial to society. On the contrary, he must admit . . . that all human life would end if his principles were to be universally accepted. All discussion and all action would immediately cease. People would become completely lethargic and would eventually perish through failing to satisfy their basic and natural needs.

But we don't need to fear such a turn of events. Human nature is always stronger than [philosophical] principles. An extreme skeptic might, through his subtle arguments, throw himself and others into a temporary amazement and confusion; but the first and most trivial event in life will make all his doubts and reservations fly away and put him in the same position, in every point of action and speculation, with the philosophers of every other sect or with those who have never concerned themselves with any philosophical issues.

When the [extreme] skeptic awakes from his dream, he will be the first to join in the laughter against himself, and he will confess that all his skeptical objections are merely amusements. Extreme skepticism

150

can do nothing but reveal the whimsical condition of the human race, who must act and reason and believe although they are not able, even through their most diligent efforts, to understand the foundations of action, or reason, or belief, or to remove the [skeptical] objections that might be raised against them.

Moderate skepticism

There is, however, a *mitigated* or *moderate* form of skepticism that might be durable and useful. This moderate skepticism arises when the excesses of extreme skepticism are corrected by common sense and [rational] reflection.

(1) Intellectual humility

The majority of people are naturally . . . certain and dogmatic in their opinions. They see the world only from one point of view and are utterly ignorant of any arguments against what they believe. They throw themselves thoughtlessly into the views that they are inclined to adopt, and they have no tolerance for those who disagree with them. Hesitation in believing or balancing one view against another confuses their understanding, undermines their enthusiasm, and stops them from acting. They can't stand any such perplexity, and they strive to escape it through their violent affirmations and obstinate beliefs. If only such people could recognize and acknowledge the limitations of the human mind . . . , they would then become more modest and reserved, lower their high opinion of themselves, and be less prejudiced against their opponents.

The uneducated should follow the example of the learned, who, in spite of all their study and reflection, are usually cautious and restrained in asserting their opinions. And if any of the learned have a tendency to be arrogant and obstinate, a small dose of skepticism might diminish their pride by showing them that the few advantages they may have attained over their fellows are really rather small when compared with the universal puzzlement and confusion that are built into human nature. In general, all the inquiries and judgments of a reasonable thinker *should always contain a certain degree of doubt, caution, and modesty.*

(2) The limitation of inquiry to accessible subjects

Another type of moderate skepticism that may be advantageous to the human race . . . is the type that would *limit our inquiries to subjects that are accessible to the narrow capacity of the human understanding.* The human imagination naturally reaches for the sublime, is delighted with whatever is remote and extraordinary, and runs uncontrollably into the most distant parts of space and time in order to avoid the things that it feels too accustomed to. Correct judgment, however, follows a contrary method: it avoids all far-out inquiries and confines itself to everyday life and to such subjects as fall under daily practice and experience. It leaves the more exalted subjects to the embellishment of poets and orators, or to the arts of priests and politicians. To bring us to such a happy position, nothing can be more useful than to appreciate the force of skeptical doubt and to recognize that nothing but the strong power of natural instinct could free us from it. Those who have an aptitude for philosophy will still continue their investigations because they realize that, besides the immediate pleasures of philosophical inquiry, philosophical judgments are nothing but the opinions of everyday life made methodical and corrected. But they will never be tempted to go beyond everyday life so long as they remember the imperfections of our mental faculties, their narrow reach, and their inaccurate operations. We can't even give a satisfactory explanation of why we believe, after a thousand experiences, that a stone will fall or that fire will burn. How, then, can we ever be satisfied with our beliefs concerning the origins of worlds and the condition of nature from and to eternity?

This . . . limitation of our investigations [to the concerns of everyday life] is completely reasonable, as we can easily see when we examine the natural powers of the human mind and compare them with their objects. We shall then discover what the proper subjects of science and [other forms of] inquiry are.

(3) The limits of certainty: two types of human knowledge

It seems to me *that quantity and number are the only subjects on which we can construct certain proofs* [demonstrations]. All attempts to extend the sphere of certain knowledge beyond these bounds are nothing but logical trickery and illusion. As the component parts of quantity and number are entirely similar, their relations are intricate and involved, and nothing is more interesting and useful than to trace, by a variety of means, their equality and inequality through their different appearances. But since all other ideas [that is, ideas other than ideas of the "component parts of quantity and number"] are clearly distinct and different from each other, no amount of intellectual analysis will enable us to do more than to observe this diversity and to assert the obvious, namely, that one thing is not another. If any difficulty *does* arise here, it proceeds entirely from the use of unclear words, which can be remedied by more exact definitions. That *the square of the hypotenuse is equal to [the sum of] the square[s] of the [other] two sides [of a right triangle]* cannot be known without a train of [mathematical] reasoning and inquiry, no matter how clearly defined the terms in the proposition are. But to prove the claim that *where there is no property there can be no injustice*, all we have to do is define injustice as a violation of property . . . . It is the same with all those pretended proofs that may be found in every branch of learning outside the sciences of quantity and number.[1] I think that it is safe to say that quantity and number are the only proper objects of demonstrative knowledge.

All other human inquiries have to do with matters of fact and existence, and these are evidently incapable of being proved. Whatever is may not be. No negation of a factual statement can be a contradiction. The nonexistence of any being, without exception, is as clear and distinct an idea as its existence. The claim that something does not exist, no matter how false that claim might be, is no less conceivable and intelligible than the claim that the thing exists. The case is different with the sciences of quantity and number. In those sciences, every statement that is not true is also confused and unintelligible. That the cube root of 64 is equal to the half of 10 is not only a false proposition, but also can never be distinctly conceived. But that Caesar or the angel Gabriel or any being never existed may be a false proposition, and yet it is perfectly conceivable and implies no contradiction.

Therefore, the existence of any being can only be proved by arguments from its cause or from its effect; and these arguments are based *completely on experience.* If we reason *a priori*, anything may appear able to produce anything. The falling of a pebble may, for all we know, extinguish the sun; or the wish of a man may control the planets in their orbits. *It is only experience that teaches us the nature and bounds of cause and effect and that enables us to infer the existence of one object from that of another.* Such is the foundation of factual reasoning, which forms the largest part of human knowledge and which is the source of all human action and behavior.

---

[1]That is, "proofs" in fields other than mathematics are merely matters of words and their definitions.

Conclusion

Factual reasoning covers either particular or general facts. Everyday discussions, history, chronology, geography, and astronomy have to do with particular facts. The sciences that consider general facts -- that is, where the qualities, causes, and effects of a whole species of objects are investigated -- are politics, natural philosophy, physics, chemistry, etc.

Theological attempts to prove the existence of God or the immortality of the soul are based partly on reasoning about particular facts and partly on reasoning about general facts. Theology has a basis in reason *insofar as it is supported by the evidence of experience*; but its best and most solid foundation is faith and divine revelation.

Ethics and aesthetics are not really matters of reasoning but rather of taste and feeling. Beauty, whether in the arts or in nature, is felt more than perceived or thought. If we *do* reason about it and try to fix the standard of beauty, we can only appeal to . . . the general taste of mankind or some such fact, and that fact may be investigated and reasoned about.

When we, as moderate skeptics, look through libraries, what havoc must we make! For example, if we pick up any volume of theology or scholastic metaphysics, we will ask, "Does it contain any abstract reasoning concerning quantity or number?" The answer will be "No." "Does it contain any experience-based reasoning about matters of fact and existence?" Again the answer will be "No." Well, then, commit it to the flames, for it can contain nothing but sophistry and illusion.

IMMANUEL KANT
(1724-1804 AD)

from the

CRITIQUE OF PURE REASON[1]

The Nature, Scope, and Limits of Human Knowledge[2]

There is no doubt that all of our knowledge (*Erkenntnis*) begins with [sense] experience (*Erfahrung*). How is our ability to

---

[1]Translated, paraphrased, and edited by George Cronk. © 1997. Kant's *Critique of Pure Reason* (*Kritik der reinen Vernunft*) is a very long, complicated, and difficult work. It was written in German and first appeared in 1781. A second edition was published in 1787. Only a few selections from the work are included in this translation, which is based on the second edition of 1787. The German text of the second edition is contained in Volume III of Kant's collected works, *Gesammelte Schriften*, 22 vols. (Berlin: Prussian Academy of Sciences, 1902-1942); the first edition is contained in Volume IV of that collection. Complete English translations of the *Critique* have been done by J.M.D. Meiklejohn in 1855 (Chicago: University of Chicago Press, "The Great Books of the Western World," Volume 42, 1952); F. Max Müller in 1881 (Garden City, NY: Dolphin Books, 2d ed., revised, 1961); and Norman Kemp Smith in 1929 (New York: St. Martin's Press, 1965).

[2]From the "Introduction" to the *Critique of Pure Reason*, B 1-24 (B 24-30 omitted). "B" denotes the second edition of the *Critique* (the first edition being designated by "A"). The numbers placed after "B" (or "A," as the case may be) refer to sections given in the Prussian Academy's *Gesammelte Schriften* (the sections corresponding to the pagination in the original German editions of the work).

know activated? Doesn't it happen in the following way? (1) The impact of [external] objects on our senses (2) gives rise to representations of these objects in our mind and also (3) stimulates our powers of understanding (*Verstand*) to compare, connect, or separate these representations in various ways thereby shaping the raw material of our sensory impressions into a knowledge of objects . . . . There is, therefore, no human knowledge prior to [sense] experience, and all such knowledge begins with [sense] experience.

Pure (*a priori*) and empirical (*a posteriori*) knowledge[1]

However, while all of our knowledge *begins with* experience, it doesn't [necessarily] follow that it all arises *out of* experience. It may be that, in addition to (1) the information we receive through sensory impressions, our empirical knowledge also contains (2) elements that our faculty of cognition supplies from itself (in which case sensory impressions may merely provide the occasion for the rise of empirical knowledge) . . . . Thus, we must carefully consider whether there is any knowledge [or any component of knowledge] that is independent of sense experience. Such knowledge is called "*a priori*," whereas empirical knowledge, which arises from and depends on experience, is called "*a posteriori*."

Now, the expression, "*a priori*," is not exact enough in and of itself to make clear the full meaning of the issue we are addressing here. Often, when we are speaking of empirical knowledge, we say that this or that general rule (which, however, we have derived from experience) may be known *a priori* because we do not derive the rule *immediately* from experience. For example, if a man were to destroy

---

[1]B 1-6.

158

the foundations of his house, we might say that he could know *a priori*, without waiting for it to happen, that the house would then collapse. Strictly speaking, however, he could not have known *a priori* (that is, without experience) that bodies [material objects] are heavy and thus that they collapse when their supports are taken away. This principle or general rule can be known only on the basis of experience [that is, *a posteriori*].

Thus, when we refer to *a priori* knowledge, we do not mean knowledge that is independent of just this or that kind of experience, but rather knowledge that is *absolutely* independent of *all* experience. When we refer to "empirical knowledge," we mean knowledge that is possible only *a posteriori*, that is, through or on the basis of [sense] experience. *A priori* knowledge, therefore, can be either "pure" or "impure." "Pure" *a priori* knowledge contains no empirical element. The proposition, "Every change has a cause," is an *a priori* proposition, but it is "impure," because the idea of change can be derived only from experience [that is, *a posteriori*] . . . .

What we need at this point is a criterion that will enable us to distinguish clearly between pure and empirical knowledge. Experience [the source of empirical knowledge] shows that a given object [of perception] is constituted in such and such a way, but experience does not show that the object could not possibly be constituted in some other way [that is, empirical judgments are not *necessarily* true] . . . . [However], if a proposition must be thought of as *necessarily* true, then it is an *a priori* judgment; and if it is not derived [by inference] from any other proposition, unless from one that is also necessarily true, then it is an **absolutely** *a priori* judgment . . . . [Furthermore], empirical judgments are never *strictly and absolutely universal* [that is, true in all conceivable cases], although such judgments are often assumed to be universally true on the basis of induction. However, the most we can say of universal judgments based on induction is that, as far as we know on the basis of our past observations, there is no exception to this or that general rule [for example, "all bodies are heavy"]. Thus, if a judgment is *strictly and absolutely universal* in that there is no possible exception to it [for example, "all triangles are three-sided"], then it is not derived from experience but is valid in an absolutely *a priori* sense . . . .

Necessity and *strict universality*, therefore, are the certain marks of pure *a priori* knowledge [as opposed to empirical knowledge, which is neither necessary nor strictly universal]. They are also inseparable from one another, but . . . [they can be used separately] since each is, by itself, an infallible criterion for distinguishing between pure and empirical knowledge . . . .

[We have now] established the fact that we have and use a mental faculty of pure *a priori* cognition, and . . . [we have also] pointed out the criteria of such cognition, namely, *necessity* and *strict universality* . . . .

The metaphysical thrust of pure reason[1]

Here is a point that is far more important than anything said so far: Some of our thinking rises completely above and beyond the sphere of any possible [sense] experience by means of concepts for which there are no corresponding objects in the empirical realm, thereby apparently extending the range of our judgments beyond the limits of experience. On this transcendental or supersensible level, where experience affords us neither instruction nor guidance, lie the investigations of [pure] reason (*Vernunft*), which, because of their importance, we consider to be far more valuable (*weit vorzüglicher*)

---

[1]B 6-10.

160

and to have a much more exalted aim than all that the understanding (*Verstand*) can accomplish in the realm of perceptible phenomena. We set such a high value on these investigations that we persist in pursuing them in spite of the risk of error, and we do not permit either doubt or disregard or indifference to detain us in that pursuit.

The unavoidable problems presented to us by pure reason are (1) [the existence of] God, (2) the freedom of the will, and (3) the immortality of the soul. The science (*Wissenschaft*) that aims at the solution of these problems is known as *metaphysics,* a science that has, until now, proceeded in a *dogmatic* manner, that is, it has confidently taken on this task [of proving the existence of God, the freedom of the will, and the immortality of the soul] without any previous investigation of the ability or inability of reason to carry out such a great undertaking.

Now, once we have left the safe ground of experience, it would seem only natural that, before we construct a building on the basis of the knowledge and principles we possess, we should first find out what the sources of that knowledge and of those principles are. Instead of trying to build without a firm foundation, it is to be expected that we should try to determine how the [human] understanding can arrive at this knowledge *a priori* and what extent, validity, and worth such knowledge may possess. The foregoing course of action would be natural if by the word "natural" we mean a procedure that is fair and reasonable; but if we mean only "that which usually happens," then nothing could be more "natural" and more comprehensible than that this inquiry [into the foundations of our *a priori* knowledge] should have been left so long unattempted.

For one part of our pure knowledge, the science of mathematics, has been for a long time very firmly established, and this fact has led us to form great expectations with regard to other aspects [of our thinking ability], though these may have a nature

161

quite different [from that of mathematical thinking]. Also, when our speculations go beyond the limits of experience, we cannot then be contradicted by experience. Moreover, the fascination of expanding the range of our knowledge is so great that, unless we are blocked by some obvious contradiction, we hurry on in our course, undisturbed by any doubts; and we can avoid any such contradiction by being careful and cautious in the construction of our fabrications (which none the less remain fabrications in spite of our maneuvers).

Mathematics is a dazzling example of how far, independently of all experience, we can extend our *a priori* knowledge. Now, the mathematician occupies himself with objects and cognitions only to the extent that they can be represented in *intuition (Anschauung)*.[1]

---

[1]Kant uses the word "intuition" frequently and in several different ways in the *Critique of Pure Reason*. According to Peter A. Angeles, "Intuitions [for Kant] are of two kinds: 1. *Empirical (a posteriori)* intuition of things by means of our sense organs, and 2. *Pure* or *formal (a priori)* intuition that structures what is given by the empirical intuition into sensations that have the quality of being in space and time." Angeles also points out that the German word for intuition, *Anschauung*, "has the connotations of 'insight,' 'perception,' 'that which is directly and immediately provided to and organized by the mind'" (*Dictionary of Philosophy* [New York: Barnes & Noble Books, 1981], p. 137). According to W.T. Jones, "[b]y 'intuition' Kant meant 'immediate and sensuous,' as opposed to 'discursive and reasoned . . . .'" (*A History of Western Philosophy (Vol. IV): Kant and the Nineteenth Century* [New York: Harcourt Brace Jovanovich, Inc., 2d ed., revised, 1975], p. 27, fn.). Frederick Copleston says that "[t]he word 'intuition' (*Anschauung*) can refer either to the act of intuiting or to what is intuited . . . ." (*A History of Philosophy*, Vol. VI [Wolfe to Kant] [Garden City, NY: Image Books, 1960], p. 235, fn.). In the section above, Kant seems to be saying that mathematics requires a kind of mental visualization of its objects and concepts. For example, the claim that space is three-dimensional requires an intuition into the structure of space. Mathematicians "intuit" their objects by representing or "constructing" them as though they were objects in space and time: "The construction, or *a priori*

But this fact is easily overlooked because this intuition can itself be given *a priori* and is therefore hard to distinguish from a pure concept (*Begriff*). Swept away by such a proof of the power of reason, we come to see no limits to the expansion of our knowledge. The light dove (*leichte Taube*), cutting through the air in free flight and feeling its resistance, might imagine that her flight would be far easier in empty space. In this way, Plato abandoned the world of the senses because of the restrictions it places on the understanding and took flight on the wings of ideas, soaring beyond the perceptible world and into the empty space of pure intellect. He did not realize that he made no real progress by all his efforts; for he met with no resistance which might, as it were, provide him a support on which he might stand and against which he might apply his powers in order to give his intellect the momentum it needed in order to progress.

It is, indeed, the common fate of human reason to complete the grand structure of speculative thought as swiftly as possible and only thereafter to ask whether the foundation is sound. Then all sorts of excuses are sought after in order to console us for the building's lack of stability, or rather, indeed, to enable us to dispense altogether with so late and dangerous an inquiry. But what frees us during the process of building from all worry or suspicion and entices us into the belief in the solidity of our construction is this: *Much or perhaps most of our reasoning consists in the analysis of concepts . . . that we already possess* [italics added]. Through such analysis, we acquire a great many insights that are prized as new forms of knowledge.

---

presentation, of a . . . triangle is analogous to the drawing of a physical triangle on a blackboard. The construction, or *a priori* presentation, of the number Two is analogous to the successive putting of one physical thing to another. Geometrical concepts are constructed in space, arithmetical in time and space" (Stephen Körner, ***Kant*** [Baltimore, MD: Penguin Books, 1955], p. 36).

163

However, these insights are really just clarifications or explanations of what was already contained in our concepts (although in a confused manner); and with regard to the matter or content thereof, we have not actually added anything to our concepts, but have only analyzed [and clarified] them. Nonetheless, this process [of analysis] does supply real *a priori* knowledge, which grows in a sure and useful way. Deceived by this, reason, without being itself aware of doing so, surreptitiously introduces assertions of a very different kind, in which it adds *a priori* to given concepts others that are completely foreign to them; and yet, we do not know how reason arrives at these *a priori* assertions, nor is the question even thought of. I shall therefore at once proceed to examine the difference between these two kinds of knowledge.

Analytic and synthetic judgments[1]

In all judgments in which we think of the relation of the subject to the predicate (I mention affirmative judgments only here; the application to negative judgments will be easily made later on), this relation is possible in two different ways. Either (1) the predicate B belongs to the subject A as something that is implicitly contained in the concept A; or (2) the predicate B lies outside of the concept A, although it does stand in connection with it [as predicate to subject]. In the first case, I call the judgment *analytic*; in the second, [I call it] *synthetic*. *Analytic* judgments (of the affirmative type), then, are those in which there is a relationship of [logical] identity between the predicate and the subject; whereas in *synthetic* judgments there is no such relationship of [logical] identity between subject and predicate.

---

[1]B 10-14.

164

Analytic judgments may [also] be called *explicative* because, in such a judgment, the predicate adds nothing to the concept of the subject, but only analyzes it into its component concepts, which were already thought of as contained in the subject, although in an unclear manner.[1] [By contrast,] synthetic judgments are *augmentative* or *ampliative* because they add to our concept of the subject a predicate that is not [logically] contained in it and that [therefore] could never be discovered merely by [logical] analysis of the concept of the subject.[2] For example, the statement, "All bodies [material objects] are extended [in space]," is an *analytic* judgment since I need not go beyond the concept of *body* in order to find extension [in space] connected with it. All I have to do is [logically] analyze the concept [of body itself], that is, become conscious of the many properties that I [must] think [are contained] in the concept [of body] in order to discover this predicate [spatial extension] in it.[3] Thus, it is an *analytic* judgment. But when I say, "All bodies are heavy," the predicate here [heavy] is something very different from that which I find in the mere concept of a body.[4] Since the foregoing statement

---

[1] That is, the predicate of an analytic proposition makes explicit (explicates) meanings that are already implicit in the subject of the proposition (for example, "a triangle is three-sided").

[2] In other words, the predicate of a synthetic proposition adds to our knowledge of the subject in a way that logical analysis, by itself, cannot (for example, "some houses are white").

[3] I cannot conceive of or imagine a material object that is not spatially extended. The idea of an unextended material object is self-contradictory.

[4] I can, without contradiction, conceive of or imagine a material object without weight (for example, a weightless object in outer space). The idea is not self-contradictory.

adds such a predicate [to the concept of the subject], it is a *synthetic* judgment.

Empirical judgments . . . are always synthetic. It would be absurd [or at least a waste of time] to think of basing an analytic judgment on experience because in forming such a judgment I need not go beyond my concepts; recourse to the testimony of experience is quite unnecessary. "Bodies are extended" is not an empirical judgment, but an *a priori* proposition. Before turning to experience, I already have in my concept [of a material object] all that is required for the judgment, and I have only to [logically] extract the predicate from the concept in accordance with the principle of contradiction and thereby . . . become conscious of the necessity of the judgment, a necessity that I could never learn from experience.

However, while I do not find the predicate *weight* in my general concept of a material object, that concept still indicates an object of experience, a part of the totality of experience, to which I can add other parts. This is what I do when I realize through observation that material objects are heavy. I can comprehend the concept [and nature] of a material object by way of [logical] analysis, which shows me that such an object must have the characteristics of extension, impenetrability, shape, etc., all of which are logically contained in the concept. But now I look back on the experience from which I have derived this concept of a material object, and I find weight at all times connected with the above [logically necessary] characteristics. Thus, I *synthetically* add *weight* as a predicate to my concept of a material object. This extends my knowledge of material objects [beyond what logical analysis alone reveals]. I can now say, "All bodies [material objects] are heavy." Therefore, the possibility of the synthesis of the predicate of weight with the concept of a material object rests on experience. Although the concept of weight is not [logically] contained in the concept of a material object, the two concepts still belong to one another (but only

166

contingently so) as parts of a whole, namely, of an experience that is itself a synthesis of intuitions.

But in **synthetic *a priori* judgments**,[1] such aid is entirely unavailable. Here, I cannot look to the sphere of experience to help me. On what basis, then, can I go beyond the concept A in order to discover that another concept B is connected with it? What can make the synthesis [of A and B] possible? Take, for example, the proposition, "Everything that happens has a cause." In the concept of "something that happens," I do think of an existing thing that is preceded by a certain period of time, and I can derive analytic judgments from this concept. But the concept of "cause" lies completely outside of and denotes something very different from "that which happens." Thus, the concept of "cause" is not [analytically] contained in the concept of "that which happens."

How then can I assert [as I do] that the concept of "cause" necessarily belongs to the concept of "that which happens"? What is the unknown *"X"* that enables the understanding to find, outside of the concept A, a predicate B that is not analytically contained in A but that is nonetheless [necessarily] connected with it? It cannot be experience because, in the proposition, "Everything that happens has a cause," the predicate is connected to the subject with greater universality than experience can ever supply and also with the character of necessity, which is completely *a priori* and based on pure concepts. All of our theoretical *a priori* knowledge aims at and rests on such synthetic (that is, augmentative) propositions. Analytic

-----

[1] A synthetic *a priori* judgment is one that is necessarily and universally true and thus not derived from experience (hence, *a priori*) and in which the predicate adds something to our knowledge of the subject that could not be known merely by logical analysis thereof.

judgments are highly important and necessary, but that is because they give us a degree of conceptual clarity that is needed for a sure and extended synthesis, which will lead to a new and real addition to the knowledge we already possess.

Examples of synthetic *a priori* judgments[1]

1. All *mathematical judgments* are synthetic. Although this is indisputably true and has very important consequences, it has until now eluded the analysts of the human mind and is, as a matter of fact, completely opposed to all their conjectures. For since it was found that all mathematical inferences proceed in accordance with the principle of contradiction (which . . . apodictic [that is, absolute] certainty requires), people became convinced that the truth of the fundamental principles of mathematics can also be known on the basis of the principle of contradiction. But here we have a fallacy. Although a synthetic proposition can be understood in accordance with the principle of contradiction, this is possible only when the proposition is validly deduced from a preceding [already known] synthetic proposition; but a synthetic proposition can never be so understood in and by itself.[2]

To begin with, we must recognize that, strictly speaking, mathematical propositions are always *a priori* judgments. They are

---

[1]B 14-18.

[2]For example, if John is a bachelor, it necessarily follows that John is unmarried. It would be contradictory to say that John is married if we knew that John is a bachelor. However, without that prior knowledge, we could not use the principle of contradiction to decide whether John is married or not. Neither of the statements, "John is unmarried" and "John is married," is, in and by itself, contradictory.

not empirical judgments because they include the concept of necessity, and necessity cannot be derived from experience. If someone objects to this, I will then limit my claim to *pure* [as opposed to applied] mathematics, the very concept of which implies that it consists only of *a priori*, non-empirical knowledge.

We might . . . at first suppose that the proposition "$7 + 5 = 12$" is a merely analytic proposition following in accordance with the principle of contradiction from the concept of a sum of 7 and 5. But if we look at it more closely, we find that our concept of the sum of 7 and 5 contains nothing more than the union of the two numbers into one; and there is, in that concept, no indication as to what the single number is which embraces both. The concept of 12 is by no means arrived at merely by thinking about the union of 7 and 5; we may analyze our concept of such a possible sum as long as we like, but still we will never find the idea of 12 in it. We must go beyond these concepts [of 7 and 5] and find an intuition that corresponds to one of them (for example, our five fingers) . . . and then, one by one, add the units contained in the five given in the intuition to the concept of 7. Starting with the number 7, and forming the concept of 5 with the aid of the fingers of my hand as objects of intuition, I now add to the number 7 the units that I previously took together to make up the number 5, and with the aid of the material image of my hand, I see the number 12 emerge. To be sure, the idea that 5 should be added to 7 was already contained in my concept of a sum equal to $7 + 5$, but . . . [the idea that said sum is equal to 12 cannot be derived analytically from the concept of $7 + 5$].

Arithmetical propositions are therefore always synthetic. We may become even more clearly convinced of this by trying larger numbers, for then it will become quite evident that, no matter how we turn and twist our concepts, it is impossible merely by conceptual analysis alone and without the aid of intuition [that is, a sensible representation, say, of numbers and equations on paper] to arrive at the number that is the sum of several large numbers.[1]

No fundamental principle of pure geometry is analytic either. "A straight line is the shortest distance between two points" is a synthetic proposition, for the concept of *straight* contains no indication of quantity, but only of quality. The concept of the *shortest* is wholly an addition, and it cannot be derived by any process of [purely logical] analysis from the concept of a straight line. Intuition, therefore, must be consulted; only by its aid is the synthesis possible.[2]

What causes us . . . to believe that the predicate of such an apodictic [absolutely certain] judgment is already contained in our concept [of the subject] and therefore that the judgment is analytic is merely the ambiguous nature of the terms we use. We believe that we *ought* to connect in thought a certain predicate [*shortest distance*] to a given subject [*straight line*], and then we imagine these concepts [of the subject and predicate] are necessarily related. However, the

---

[1]"[W]e cannot carry on any even fairly elaborate reasoning in mathematics without, as it were, placing ourselves at the mercy of a symbolic representation. Prior to the construction of a proof or calculation [on paper, chalkboard, etc.] we do not know the answer to any substantial mathematical question." This is why Kant asserts "that mathematics proceeds by representing concepts in intuition . . ." (Charles Parsons, "Foundations of Mathematics," in *The Encyclopedia of Philosophy*, ed. Paul Edwards, Volume 5 [New York: Macmillan Publishing Co., Inc., 1967], p. 198).

[2]Does this mean that we must mentally visualize (perhaps with the assistance of physical representations) two points in space and the various lines that may be drawn between them in order to "see" that the shortest such line is a straight one?

question is not what we *ought* to join to the given subject, but what we *actually find* in it, even if only obscurely. Then it becomes clear that the predicate is necessarily connected to the subject, not by the force of logic, but rather by virtue of a sensible intuition that must be added to the concept of the subject.[1]

Some few fundamental propositions presupposed by geometricians are, indeed, truly analytic and depend on the principle of contradiction. However, like identical propositions, they serve only as links in the chain of method and not as principles -- for example, "$a = a$," the whole is equal to itself; or "$(a + b) > a$," the whole is greater than its part. And even these propositions, which are valid in a purely logical sense, are only recognized in mathematics because they can be represented in [sensible] intuition.

2. *Natural Science* [Kant is thinking here mainly of *physics*] also contains synthetic *a priori* judgments as principles. I shall cite two such scientific judgments: (1) "In all changes of the material world, the quantity of matter remains unchanged"; and (2) "In all communication of motion, action and reaction must always be equal." In both of these, not only is their necessity and therefore their *a priori* origin clear, but it is also clear that they are synthetic propositions. With regard to (1), there is nothing in the [bare] concept of matter that logically requires me to conceive of its unchanging quantity (*Beharrlichkeit*), although I *am* logically required to think of it as present in and filling space. I therefore really must go beyond the concept of matter in order to think *on to it*

---

[1]This paragraph is attached as part of the following paragraph in the original German text, but various scholars, including Kemp Smith, believe that it should precede "Some few fundamental propositions . . . represented in [sensible] intuition."

something *a priori* that I am not logically required to think *in it*. Proposition (1) is therefore not analytic, but synthetic; and yet it is . . . *a priori*. This is also true with regard to the other propositions of the pure part of natural science.

3. As to *metaphysics*, even if we consider it to be thus far an unsuccessful science, it is nonetheless an indispensable one owing to the nature of human reason,[1] and it ought to contain synthetic *a priori* propositions. Metaphysics should not merely dissect and analyze the concepts of things that we form *a priori*. No, it should *expand* the range of our *a priori* knowledge. For this purpose, we must find principles that can add to a given concept something that was not already [logically] contained in it and, by means of synthetic *a priori* judgments, move well beyond the limits of experience, as, for example, in such propositions as, "the world must have a beginning." Metaphysics, then, at least in terms of what it aims at, consists of nothing but synthetic *a priori* propositions.

The general problem of pure reason[2]

. . . The proper problem of pure reason, then, is expressed in the question, "How are synthetic *a priori* judgments possible?"

That metaphysics has thus far remained in such an unresolved state of uncertainty and contradiction is a result of the fact that this great problem, and perhaps even the difference between analytic and synthetic judgments, did not before now suggest itself to

---

[1]That is, human reason, by its very nature, cannot resist the tendency to ask and seek answers to metaphysical questions.

[2]B 19-24.

172

philosophers. The very existence or downfall of metaphysics depends on the solution of this problem -- or on a clear proof of the impossibility of synthetic *a priori* knowledge.

Of all [previous] philosophers, David Hume came closest to recognizing [and appreciating the importance of] this problem; but it never became clear enough in his mind, nor did he grasp the issue in its totality. He concentrated only on the synthetic proposition concerning the connection of an effect with its cause . . . [that is, "There is a necessary connection between cause and effect"], and he insisted that it is impossible for such a proposition to be true *a priori*. According to Hume, metaphysics is a mere delusion arising from our fanciful belief that we have rational insight into that which is actually borrowed from experience and which, on the basis of habit and custom, has taken on a misleading appearance of necessity. If Hume had grasped our problem in its totality, he would not have drawn such a conclusion, which is destructive to all pure philosophy [metaphysics]. For he would then have recognized that, according to his own argument, there could also be no pure mathematics (which must certainly contain synthetic *a priori* propositions) -- an absurdity from which his good sense would have saved him.

In pursuing a solution of the above problem, we must also decide whether it is possible to use pure reason to establish and construct all such sciences that contain theoretical *a priori* knowledge of objects. We must therefore also answer the following questions: (1) How is pure mathematical science possible?, and (2) How is pure natural science possible?

Since such sciences do certainly exist, it is proper to ask how they are possible. That they *are* possible is shown by the fact that they do really exist. However, with regard to metaphysics, the fact that it has thus far made such miserable progress and the fact that no system has yet been developed that has fulfilled the purpose of metaphysics leaves a very reasonable doubt as to the very possibility of the existence [of such a science].

Yet, in a certain sense, metaphysical knowledge must unquestionably be looked upon as given; that is, metaphysics must be considered to really exist, if not as a science, nevertheless as a *natural disposition* of the human mind. For human reason, not on the basis of any merely vain desire for great knowledge, but rather driven on by its own deeply felt need and impetus, raises questions that cannot be answered by any empirical application of reason or by any principles derived therefrom. Thus, there has always existed in every man some kind of metaphysics. Metaphysics will always exist as long as [human] reason realizes that it has a power of speculation and that it is able to exercise that power.

At this point, another question arises: "How is metaphysics, as a natural disposition, possible?" Pure reason poses metaphysical questions to itself and is impelled by its own need to answer such questions as well as it can. We want to know exactly how such questions arise from the nature of . . . human reason.

In all past attempts to answer the [metaphysical] questions which reason is moved by its very nature to ask itself -- for example, whether the world had a beginning or has existed from all eternity -- reason has always run into unavoidable contradictions. We must not rest content with the mere natural inclination of the mind to engage in metaphysical speculation, that is, with the mere existence of the faculty of pure reason from which, to be sure, some sort of metaphysical system always arises. What we want is a definite answer to the question whether we do or do not know the objects of metaphysics. We want to decide either what the proper objects of metaphysical thought are or whether reason is able or unable to pass any judgment on them, so that we may either extend with confidence the boundaries of pure reason or set strictly defined and safe limits to its action. Thus, our last question, which arises out of the general problem stated above ["How are synthetic *a priori* judgments possible?"], is, "How is metaphysics as a science possible?"

Thus, the *critique* of [pure] reason, at last, leads both naturally and necessarily to scientific knowledge, whereas the *dogmatic* [uncritical] use of pure reason results in groundless claims against which other equally groundless claims can always be opposed, thus pushing us inevitably into skepticism.

Metaphysics as science shouldn't be overly abstract and complicated because it is not concerned with the objects of reason (of which there is an inexhaustible variety), but merely with reason itself and with the problems that arise entirely from within reason itself, problems that are not imposed upon reason by anything outside itself, but rather by its own nature. Once reason has come to completely understand its own power with regard to objects presented to it in experience, it will find it easy to determine with certainty the extent and limits of its attempted application to objects that stand beyond the boundaries of experience.

We may and must, therefore, consider all previous attempts to establish metaphysics on a dogmatic basis as failures. The analytic aspect of any such attempt, that is, the mere dissection of concepts that inhere *a priori* in our reason, is only a preparation for and not at all the aim of metaphysics in the true sense, the purpose of which is the extension of our synthetic *a priori* knowledge. For this purpose, mere analysis is useless because it only shows what is contained in our concepts, not how we arrive at them *a priori*; and this is what metaphysics must show in order to determine the correct use of these concepts with regard to the objects of all knowledge in general.

Only a little self-denial is needed to give up the pretensions [of dogmatic metaphysics], seeing that the undeniable (and, in the dogmatic mode of procedure, also unavoidable) contradictions of reason with itself have long since undermined the authority of every metaphysical system that has appeared up to this time. We will need to be very firm to remain undeterred (by difficulty from within and by opposition from without) from trying, by a method completely different from all those followed in the past, to further the growth and fruitfulness of a science indispensable to human reason -- a science whose every branch may be cut off, but whose roots remain indestructible . . . .

* * * * * * * * * *

Editor's Comment

Kant's solution to the general problem of pure reason, that is, his answer to the question, "How are synthetic *a priori* judgments possible?," may be summarized as follows:[1] There are two sources of human knowledge, namely, sensibility (*Sinnlichkeit*) and understanding (*Verstand*). The power of sensibility enables us to have sensations of objects external to ourselves, which we perceive as located in space and time. Our sensibility then presents these objects to the mind, and the mental power of understanding supplies a set of concepts (which Kant calls the "categories of the understanding") through which we are enabled to think about and comprehend said objects. Thus, Kant sees knowledge as a joint

---

[1]For Kant's full presentation, see B 31-349. This section encompasses Kant's "I. Transcendental Doctrine of Elements," First Part, "Transcendental Aesthetic" (on space and time), and Second Part, "Transcendental Logic," "Introduction" and First Division, "Transcendental Analytic" (on the categories of the understanding).

product of sensory experience and the mind's shaping of the evidence of experience into comprehensible form.

Space and time, according to Kant, do not have an objective existence; they are part of our perceptual apparatus -- he calls them the *forms* of sensibility -- and through them, we are able to "intuit" objects of sensation. Similarly, the categories of the understanding are subjective, part of our mental constitution. The forms of sensibility (space and time) and the categories of the understanding, which constitute the innate and therefore *a priori* structure of human consciousness, dictate the ways in which we *must* perceive and think about the world. Thus, the objects that we perceive (through the forms of sensible intuition, space and time) and think about (through the categories of the understanding) must conform to the innate and *a priori* constitution of the mind. How we experience and understand the world is a result of the way in which the mind is structured and of how it works.

Instead of assuming that the mind conforms to its objects (an assumption that he attributed to all prior thinkers), Kant assumed that the objects of consciousness conform to the structure and operations of the mind itself. He claimed that the mind is so structured as to *legislate* the manner in which the world of sense experience *must* appear to us. The mind does not *discover* the order of nature but rather *imposes* its own order *on* nature.

Kant thought of his theory of the relation between consciousness and its objects as bringing about a revolution in philosophy comparable to the 16th century Copernican revolution in astronomy. The following is a famous passage from Kant's "Preface" to the second edition of the ***Critique of Pure Reason***:[1]

> It has hitherto been assumed that our thought must conform to the objects [that exist in the external world]; but, as a result of this assumption, all attempts to understand these objects *a priori* . . . and thus to extend the range of our knowledge have been failures. Perhaps, then, we will be more successful in our metaphysical efforts if we instead assume that objects must conform to [the structure of] our thought. This would seem to . . . [increase our chances] of arriving at *a priori* knowledge of objects, that is, of knowing something about these objects before they appear to us in experience. We propose to do [in philosophy] exactly what Copernicus did [in astronomy] in his attempt to explain the movements of the heavenly bodies. When he found that he could not succeed on the basis of the traditional assumption that all the heavenly bodies revolved around the spectator [on earth], he turned the tables and adopted the assumption that the spectator [on earth] revolves while the stars [such as the sun in our solar system] remain at rest. *We may make the same move in metaphysics with regard to our intuition of objects. If intuition must conform to the structure of its objects, I don't see how we can acquire any a priori knowledge of them. If, however, objects (that is, objects of the senses) must conform to the structure of our faculty of intuition, I can then easily see that a priori knowledge [of empirical objects] is possible. Now, for the objects of intuition to become known, they must appear to the mind as representations of something external to the mind, and the mind must then determine just what these objects are. Here, there are two ways to go: either (1) we may assume that the concepts by which we determine the nature of the objects of intuition conform to the objects themselves; or (2) we may assume that the objects of intuition . . . conform to [the structure of] our concepts. Option (1) keeps us in the dark as to how any a priori knowledge of the objects of experience is possible. But*

---

[1]B xvi-xviii.

178

option (2) gives us more hope.[1] For experience itself is a form of knowledge that includes understanding; and understanding contains *a priori* rules that are in my mind before objects are given to me [by the senses]. These rules are expressed in *a priori* concepts to which all the objects of experience must conform and with which they must agree. Now, there are objects contemplated by reason (*Vernunft*) [as opposed to the understanding (*Verstand*)] that cannot appear in experience, or, at least, cannot appear in the way in which reason characterizes them. Reason cannot resist thinking about such non-appearing objects [for example, God]. The attempt [by reason] to comprehend these ["transcendental"] objects will provide an excellent test of our new method of thought, which is based on the principle that our *a priori* knowledge of things is only a knowledge of that which we ourselves put into them.

Sensibility (or sensible intuition) presents objects to us under the forms of space and time. We can't experience objects in any other way. Then the mind categorizes and conceptualizes these

---

[1]The italicized passage above is very loosely translated. The German text reads: *"In der Metaphysik kann man nun, was die Anschauung der Gegenstände betrifft, es auf ähnliche Weise versuchen. Wenn die Anschauung sich nach der Beschaffenheit der Gegenstände richten müßte, so sehe ich nicht ein, wie man a priori von ihr etwas wissen könne; richtet sich aber der Gegenstand (als Objekt der Sinne) nach der Beschaffenheit unseres Anschauungsvermögens, so kann ich mir diese Möglichkeit ganz wohl vorstellen. Weil ich aber bei diesen Anschauungen, wenn sie Erkenntnisse werden sollen, nicht stehen bleiben kann, sondern sie als Vorstellungen auf irgend etwas als Gegenstand beziehen und diesen durch jene bestimmen muß, so kann ich entweder annehmen, die Begriffe, wodurch ich diese Bestimmung zustande bringe, richten sich auch nach dem Gegenstande, und denn bin ich wiederum in derselben Verlegenheit wegen der Art, wie ich a priori hievon etwas wissen könne; oder ich nehme an, die Gegenstände oder, welches einerlei ist, die Erfahrung, in welcher sie allein (als gegebene Gegenstände) erkannt werden, richte sich nach diesen Begriffen, so sehe ich sofort eine leichtere Auskunft . . . . "* (B xvii).

179

objects by means of the power of understanding. There are twelve categories of the understanding, and they are divided into four sets of three each, as follows:

Table of Categories[1]

I
Of Quantity
Unity (or Singularity)
Plurality (or Particularity)
Totality (or Universality)

II
Of Quality
Reality (or Affirmation)
Negation
Limitation

III
Of Relation
Substance-Attribute
Cause-and-Effect
Community (or Reciprocity between Agent and Patient)

IV
Of Modality
Possibility-Impossibility
Existence-Nonexistence
Necessity-Contingency

When an object is presented to the mind in sensible intuition, it necessarily appears in space and time, since these "forms of sensibility" are *a priori* structures of consciousness. The mind then

---

[1] Adapted from Kant's "Table of Categories," B 106.

180

comes to comprehend the object by applying the categories of the understanding to it, and the object must conform to these *a priori* conceptual structures. The mind must, by its nature, make a judgment (or set of judgments) about the object by using the categories of *quantity*, *quality*, *relation*, and *modality*, and the object must submit itself to the application of these categories.

Suppose I perceive a white cat. If I think about it, I can (depending on my empirical experience of the cat) say the following: (1) *As to quantity*: This object I am perceiving is a *single* white cat (singular judgment under the category of unity). Of all cats, only *some* are white (particular judgment under the category of plurality), but *all* cats are animals (universal judgment under the category of totality). (2) *As to quality*: This object *is* a white cat (affirmative judgment under the category of reality or affirmation); it *is not* a black dog (negative judgment under the category of negation); and I can't say whether it is or isn't a stray (limitative judgment under the category of limitation, which states that it is, at least at the moment, impossible to affirm or negate a quality of this object). (3) *As to relation*: This *cat* (substance) is *white* (attribute) (under the category of substance-attribute); its hunger (or something else) has *caused* it to be here before me (causal judgment under the category of cause-and-effect); and this cat is *here now*, coexisting and interacting with me, looking to me for food, etc. (under the category of community or interaction between agent and patient). (4) *As to modality* (which refers to an object's manner of existence or nonexistence): This cat's existence is *possible* (under the category of possibility-impossibility) because it does, in fact, *exist* (under the category of existence-nonexistence), but it has only *contingent* (as opposed to necessary) existence since its nonexistence is logically possible, that is, the thought of its nonexistence is not a contradiction in terms (under the category of necessity-contingency).

181

That the object before me is a white cat, etc., is empirically determined (that is, *a posteriori*), but that the object must appear in space and time and that it must be subject to judgment on the basis of the categories of the understanding is knowable *a priori* because space and time and the categories are innate features of the mind's apparatus. Thus, for example we can know *a priori* (that is, with necessity and universality) (1) that the shortest distance between two points is a straight line and (2) that all events are caused because (1) the space of human sensibility is Euclidean space and because (2) all events that appear to us in space and time must be subsumed under the mind's innate category of cause-and-effect (not to mention the other eleven categories of the understanding). And yet, according to Kant, these judgments are synthetic, not analytic (because their predicates are not logically contained in their subjects) -- they are synthetic *a priori* propositions.[1]

Kant argues further that the categories of the understanding are applicable only to objects that appear to us under the forms of sensibility. They are not applicable to "transcendental objects" that do not appear in space and time (for example, God, the world as a cosmic totality, the self, freedom of the will, the immortality of the soul). Human knowledge, for Kant, is confined to the world that appears to us in sense experience, which he calls the world of *phenomena*. We cannot have knowledge of anything that transcends our experience. Anything that lies beyond our experience (for example, an object as it *really* is, apart from our experience, the "thing-in-itself" [*Ding an sich*]) also lies beyond the reach of our understanding. Kant calls such transcendental realities *noumena*. Since noumena do not appear in our experience (that is, in space and

---

[1]See above, pp. 167-168 and 170-171.

182

time), they cannot be subsumed under the categories of the understanding.

In spite of this limitation on human knowledge, reason (*Vernunft*) inevitably thinks beyond the phenomenal realm and formulates *ideas* of "transcendental" realities in an effort to account for the coherence of phenomenal experience. How can my experience be as orderly and unified as it is if there is no unified and substantial self ("I") to serve as experiencer? How can the objects of my experience behave in such orderly and predictable ways if there is no "world-in-itself" as a cosmic totality that causes me to have the experiences I have? How could either the world or I begin to exist at all if there is no God to cause and sustain our existence? In raising and pursuing answers to these questions, reason tends to affirm the existence of the **self**, the **world** as a unified totality, and **God**, which Kant calls the "transcendental ideas of pure reason." If we *assume* (but without actually *asserting*) the existence of (1) a substantial self, (2) the cosmos as a totality, and (3) God, we can then explain (1) the unity of subjective experience, (2) the apparently systematic order of the world that appears phenomenally to us in experience, and (3) the existence and systematic unity of the entire field of experience. This transcendental tendency of pure reason, so long as it leads only to *belief* in the existence of self, world, and God and does not mislead us into thinking that we can have *knowledge* of these transcendental realities, may, in fact, serve a useful scientific and philosophical purpose.

At this point, let's return to reading Kant and letting him speak for himself.

183

The Transcendental Ideas of Pure Reason[1]

Self, Cosmos, and God[2]

The [transcendental] ideas of pure reason [self, cosmos, God] can never be dialectical[3] in themselves; any deceptive illusion to which they give rise must be due solely to their misemployment. For these ideas emerge from the very nature of our reason; and it is impossible that this supreme court of all the rights and claims of speculation should be the source of deceptions and illusions. We must assume that the [transcendental] ideas have a good and proper job to perform as determined by the natural disposition of human reason . . . .

If the [transcendental] ideas of pure reason are to have any objective validity . . . and are not to be viewed as merely empty mental constructions . . . , a justification of them must be possible . . . .

There is a big difference between something being presented to the mind as an *object in the absolute sense* and its being presented

---

[1]From B 697-732, "Of the Ultimate End of the Natural Dialectic of Human Reason," which is a part of the "Appendix" to "I. Transcendental Doctrine of Elements," Second Part, "Transcendental Logic," Second Division, "Transcendental Dialectic."

[2]B 697-701.

[3]Kant uses the term "dialectic" as a name for the misguided effort of reason to apply the principles governing phenomena (the forms of sensibility and the categories of the understanding) to the transcendental realm of noumena. This is not a standard use of the term.

184

merely as an *ideal object*. In the former case, our concepts [that is, the categories of the understanding] are employed to identify and comprehend the object; whereas in the latter case, there is [in the mind] only an abstract prototype ("schema") to which no object of experience corresponds or *can* correspond and which only enables us to represent to ourselves other objects in a mediate and indirect manner by means of their relation to this ideal object. [For example,] the idea of a supreme intelligence [God] is a *mere* idea . . . [since] we have no way of establishing the existence of its object [because God, the object of this idea, does not appear in the phenomenal world]. [The idea of God] is only a schema [mental prototype, abstract idea] of a thing in general, constructed in accordance with reason's demand for the highest possible degree of systematic unity (*systematische Einheit*) in . . . [our experience of the world].[1] On this basis, we regard the objects of experience as effects

---

[1]Kant holds that reason, by its nature, strives to organize all of our judgements about the phenomenal world into a coherent, unified system (or "systematic unity"). For example, the various judgments, "All Greeks are mortal," "All Romans are mortal," "All Indians are mortal," etc., can be unified under the more general judgment, "All humans are mortal," and that judgment, along with "All cats are mortal," "All dogs are mortal," "All rabbits are mortal," etc., can be unified under the even more general judgment, "All animals are mortal," and so on. (1) "All animals are mortal" is a condition of the truth of (2) "All humans are mortal," which, in turn, is a condition of the truth of (3) "All Greeks are mortal." In subsuming (3) under (2) and then (2) under (1), reason is not content to stop the process at (1), but seeks to push on in pursuit of that which is completely unconditioned. As Kant puts it, reason tries "to find the unconditioned condition, whereby the unity of the conditioned knowledge obtained through the understanding is brought to completion" (B 364). In this way, reason seeks an ever greater unification and systematization of knowledge by proceeding *as if* the foundations of knowledge were the absolute and unconditioned unities of the self, the world as a whole, and God -- none of which appears as an object of experience in the phenomenal world.

185

caused by God, the purported object of the idea of a supreme intelligence, and who is viewed as the ground or cause of the objects of experience. In other words, the transcendental idea of a supreme intelligence leads us to view the things of the world *as if* (*als ob*) they received their existence from a supreme intelligence. The idea, therefore, does not point to, or prove the existence of, its object, but is rather a useful hypothesis that can give meaningful direction to our investigations of the world. It doesn't show how objects are constituted, but it does indicate how, under its guidance, we should go about investigating the constitution and relations of objects in the world of experience.

Now, if it can be shown that the three transcendental ideas (the psychological [self], the cosmological [cosmos], and the theological [God]), although they do not point to any objects in the world of experience, can nevertheless, on the assumption that the objects of these ideas [self, cosmos, and God] exist, give systematic unity to reason in its empirical investigations and thereby enable us to extend our empirical knowledge without ever contradicting or opposing it, then it is a necessary maxim of reason to proceed in accordance with these ideas. This, then, is the [justification] of the ideas of [pure] speculative reason: They are not *constitutive* principles that bring us to knowledge of more objects than can be given in experience, but, as *regulative* principles [that guide our reasoning about the world], they do give systematic unity to our empirical knowledge.[1] In this way, our empirical knowledge is arranged and improved within its

---

[1]When Kant says that a principle is "constitutive," he means that it refers to an actual object of knowledge in the phenomenal world. When he describes a principle as "regulative," he means that it designates only an ideal (not an actual or empirical) object, which, however, is useful in guiding or "regulating" our study of the world.

own limits to a greater extent than would be possible through the employment merely of the principles of the understanding alone (that is, without the aid of the transcendental ideas).

I shall try to make this more clear. If we reason in accordance with the principles implied in the transcendental ideas, we shall, *first*, in psychology, connect [and unify] all of the inward appearances, actions, and feelings of consciousness *as if* the mind were a simple[1] substance with a personal identity that persists [through time] (in this life at least), while its various states, as well as the states of the body (which are external to the mind), are continually changing. *Secondly*, in cosmology, [the idea of the cosmos as a unified causal series of events] stimulates the mind to investigate the conditions that give rise to both internal and external natural phenomena *as if* these conditions and phenomena belong to an infinitely long [causal] series, without any first or supreme member (in which case our causal investigations will never be completed) . . . . [2] *Thirdly*, in theology, [the idea of God] leads us to view everything in the realm of possible experience *as if* it forms an absolute . . . [systematic] unity and, at the same time, *as if* it (the empirical world) stands on a single, supreme, and all-sufficient ground beyond itself, that is, on a self-subsistent, primordial, [and] creative reason [God]. Guided by this idea, reason seeks its fullest comprehension of the empirical

---

[1] That is, unified and uncompounded.

[2] Kant's point here seems to be that the transcendental idea of the cosmos as a totality encompassing an infinitely long causal series (that is, not a closed or completed totality) is a stimulus to scientific investigation, science being, in part at least, a search for the causal conditions that produce the phenomena of experience.

187

world by viewing all objects of experience *as if* they were grounded on such an archetype . . . . [1]

More on the transcendental idea of the Self[2]

The first [idea of pure reason] points to the "I" itself, viewed simply as a thinking substance or soul . . . . Reason, beginning with the . . . [apparent] empirical unity of all thought, and thinking of this unity as unconditioned and original, constructs from it . . . the idea of a substantial self: that is, the idea of a simple substance (1) that is unchangeable in itself, (2) that has a personal identity that persists through time, and (3) that exists in relation to other real things outside it -- in a word, the idea of a simple self-subsisting intelligence. However, the only purpose that reason has here is to find a principle of systematic unity that will enable it to explain the apparent unity of phenomenal experience. It is trying to present (1) all determinations of the inner sense as existing in a single subject, (2) all powers [of perception and thought] . . . as derived from a single fundamental power, (3) all changes as belonging to the states of one and the same permanent being,

---

[1] According to Frederick Copleston, "the transcendental Idea of God as a supreme intelligence and the cause of the universe leads us to think of Nature as a systematic teleological unity. And this presupposition aids the mind in its investigation of Nature.... [I]f we think of Nature *as if* it were...an intelligent work of an intelligent author, we shall be prompted, in Kant's opinion, to carry on the work of scientific investigation by subsumption under causal laws.... The idea of Nature as the work of an intelligent creator involves the idea of Nature as an intelligible system. And this presupposition is a spur to scientific investigation...." (*A History of Philosophy*, Vol. VI [Wolfe to Kant] [Garden City, NY: Image Books, 1960], p. 303).

[2] B 710-712.

188

and (4) all phenomena in space as entirely different from the activity of thought. In this process, reason applies simplicity and other attributes of the category of substance to the self only in a regulative sense [that is, as a rule of procedure].[1] Reason does not assume that the category of substance is the actual ground of the attributes of the soul, for these attributes may rest on completely different grounds of which we know nothing. These [regulatively] assumed attributes cannot reveal to us the soul as it is in itself, not even if we regarded them as valid in respect of it, for they constitute a mere idea which cannot be represented *in concreto* [that is, in the phenomenal world] . . . .

[Thus,] . . . reason's investigations [with regard to the transcendental self] . . . [are] directed to reducing the grounds of explanation in the field [of empirical experience], as much as is possible, to a single principle. This is best attained through . . . [the idea of the self] viewed *as if* it were a real being; indeed, this reduction cannot be attained in any other way.

The psychological idea [that is, the transcendental idea of the self] is [therefore] nothing but a rule ("schema") for applying a regulative concept [to our inner experience in order to give that experience systematic unity]. If I ask, "Does the *soul-in-itself* have a spiritual nature?," the question has no meaning. *In thinking of the soul as a spiritual being, I construct in my mind an abstract object that does not appear in the world of nature. Such an object can have none of the predicates of any possible experience, and therefore it cannot be conceptualized as an object under the categories of the*

---

[1]Does this mean that, if the self were an object of experience (which it isn't), it could then be brought under the category of substance and perhaps the other categories of the understanding?

189

understanding. But since the idea of an object can have meaning only if the object itself appears in the phenomenal world, the idea of the soul as a spiritual being is meaningless.[1]

More on the transcendental idea of the Cosmos[2]

The second . . . [transcendental idea of pure reason] is the idea of the world-in-general [that is, as the totality of all empirically discernible causal sequences] . . . . There are two kinds of nature: thinking nature [mind] and material nature [matter]. To think about material nature . . . , that is, to apply the categories [of the understanding] to it, we need no [transcendental] idea, no idea of anything that transcends experience. In fact, no [transcendental] idea is possible in this context since in thinking about material nature we are guided solely by sensible intuition. The situation here is different from that of the fundamental [and transcendental] idea of psychology (the "I"), which contains *a priori* a certain form of thought, namely, the unity of the "I." Thus, there remains for pure reason nothing to deal with but nature in general and the completeness of its conditions in accordance with some principle.

The [idea of the] absolute totality of the series of these conditions determining the derivation of all their members [that is, the totality of all the causal sequences in nature] . . . is an idea that

---

[1]This italicized passage is very loosely translated. Kant's actual words are, "*Denn durch einen solchen Begriff nehme ich nicht bloß die körperliche Natur, sondern überhaupt alle Natur weg, d. i. alle Prädikate irgend einer möglichen Erfahrung, mithin alle Bedingungen, zu einem solchen Begriffe einen Gegenstand zu denken, als welches doch einzig und allein es macht, daß man sagt, er habe einen Sinn*" (B 712).

[2]B 712-713.

can never be connected to an object through the empirical exercise of reason. However, the idea can serve as a rule that tells us how to proceed in dealing with such causal series: that is, in seeking [causal] explanations of phenomena (whether in regressing or ascending order), we ought to treat a [causal] series *as if* it were in itself infinite, that is, *as if* it proceeded *in indefinitum* [without definite beginning or end] . . . . [1]

More on the transcendental idea of God[2]

The third [transcendental] idea of pure reason, which merely hypothesizes the existence of a single and sufficient cause of all cosmological series, is the idea of *God*. We have no basis whatever for assuming that the object of this idea actually exists in itself, for how can we believe in or assert the existence of a necessary and supremely perfect being merely on the basis of an idea in the mind; and if we did adopt such a belief or make such an assertion, how could we justify our procedure? The only way to show that the supposition of God's existence is necessary is to show that the idea of the world as a connected and systematic unity depends on the truth of this supposition, that is, to show that we are required to look at the world *as if* all such connection and unity is grounded in one single all-embracing being, which is the supreme and all-sufficient cause [of the world] . . . .

This highest formal unity, which is based on ideas alone, is the *purposive* unity (*zweckmäßige Einheit*) of things. The *theoretical* interest of reason makes it necessary to regard all order in the world

---

[1]See the second footnote on p. 187, above.

[2]B 713-717 and 721-729.

191

as if it had originated from the intention and design of a supreme reason. Such a perspective leads reason to completely new views in the field of experience as to how the things of the world may be connected in accordance with teleological laws and thus to reach their greatest systematic unity. Thus, the hypothesis of a supreme intelligence as the one and only cause of the universe -- as long as we attribute to such a being a merely hypothetical and ideal existence -- is always beneficial and never harmful to reason.

If, then, in studying the shape of the earth . . . or of the mountains or the seas, we presuppose wise designs on the part of an author of the universe, we are enabled to make in this way a number of discoveries. Provided that we limit ourselves to a merely regulative use of this hypothesis, even error cannot do us much harm. For the worst that can happen would be that where we expected to find a teleological connection . . . we find only a mechanical or physical connection . . . . In such a case, we merely fail to find the additional form of unity we expected; we do not lose the unity reason insists upon in its empirical investigations.

A disappointment like this cannot undermine the general utility of the teleological law itself. For example, an anatomist is guilty of error when he claims that some part of an animal's body serves a purpose that it clearly does not serve; but it is quite impossible to prove in any given case that an arrangement of nature, whatever it may be, serves no purpose whatsoever. Thus, [the science of] medical physiology, acting on the basis of the [transcendental] teleological principle supplied by pure reason, carries this principle so far as to assume with great confidence, and with approval of all intelligent people, that every organ or bodily part of an animal has its use and serves some good purpose. In this way, the physiologist expands his very limited knowledge of the purposive functioning of organic bodies.

If the God hypothesis (and the teleological principle that goes along with it) is treated as constitutive [that is, as *proving* that there are divinely-originated purposes in nature], then we are going way beyond what can be justified on the basis of observation. We must therefore conclude that this hypothesis is nothing more than a regulative principle of reason. This principle leads us on to the highest degree of systematic unity [in our view of the world] by grounding that unity in the idea of a purposive causality in the supreme cause of the world -- *as if* this being, as supreme intelligence and acting in accordance with a supremely wise design, were the cause of all things.

If, however, we overlook this restriction of the idea [of God] to a merely regulative use, then reason is led astray. For it then leaves the ground of experience, which alone can . . . mark out its proper course, and ventures out beyond it into the incomprehensible and unfathomable, rising to dizzying heights where it finds itself entirely cut off from all possible action in conformity with experience . . . .

To take the regulative principle of the systematic unity of nature as being a constitutive principle and to attribute actual existence to a cause that serves merely as a guiding idea . . . for the consistent and harmonious exercise of reason will involve us in unavoidable confusions. The investigation of nature follows its own course, explaining phenomena on the basis of natural causes in accordance with the general laws of nature. It is true that the investigation of nature is guided by the idea of an author of the universe -- not, however, in order to deduce the purposiveness for which it is always looking from this Supreme Being, but rather in order to deduce the existence of such a Being from the purposiveness of nature. By seeking this purposiveness in the phenomena of nature, the investigation of nature seeks, if possible, to know the existence of this Supreme Being as absolutely necessary. Whether this enterprise can succeed or not, the idea [of God] remains always true in itself and justified in its use, provided that it is employed only as a regulative principle.

Complete purposive unity constitutes absolute perfection. If we do not find this unity in the empirical world nor in the universal and necessary laws of nature, how, then, can we infer from this unity the idea of a supreme and absolutely necessary perfection of a primordial being as the origin of all causality? The greatest possible systematic unity (and thus also purposive unity) is the very foundation of the possibility of reason's greatest possible employment. The idea of such unity is, therefore, essentially and inseparably associated with the very nature of reason itself. For this reason, the idea of complete purposive unity is *legislative* for us [that is, it requires us, as a matter of law, to see the world as a complete systematic unity]. Thus, it is only natural for us to assume the existence of a higher legislative reason corresponding to our own, from which the systematic unity of nature is derived . . . .

If, then, in connection with such a transcendental theology, we ask, *first*, whether there is anything distinct from the world that contains [or is] the foundation of the [systematic] order and connection of nature in accordance with universal laws, the answer is *Yes, without a doubt!* For the world is an aggregate of phenomena; and there must . . . be some transcendental foundation of these phenomena, a foundation which is thinkable by the pure understanding alone (*bloß dem reinen Verstande denkbarer*).[1]

---

[1]Kant uses the term "understanding" (*Verstand*) here. To be consistent with his own usage, should he have used the word "reason" (*Vernunft*) instead?

194

If, *secondly*, we ask whether this [transcendental] being is a *substance*, whether it *really exists*, whether it has *necessary existence*, and so on, the reply is that *this question is completely meaningless*. For all categories [of the understanding] through which we might try to conceptualize such an object are applicable only to *phenomena* [and not at all to *noumena*]. The categories [such as *substance, reality, existence, necessity*] have no meaning at all when they are applied to objects that cannot appear in experience, that is, in the sensible world (*Sinnenwelt*). Outside of the sphere of sensation, the categories are nothing but names for concepts . . . through which [by themselves, without the aid of experience] we can understand nothing.

If, *thirdly*, we ask whether we may think of this being [God], which is distinct from the world, by way of *analogy* with the objects of experience, the answer is, *Certainly, but only as an ideal object and not a real one*. That is, we must think of it only as an unknown substratum of the systematic unity, order, and purposiveness (*Zweckmäßigkeit*) of the world -- a regulative idea that gives direction to reason in its investigation of nature . . . . What this primordial ground of the unity of the world is *in itself*, we cannot know; we can only know how to use it (or rather the idea of it) to guide reason in its systematic investigation of the world of experience . . . .

Therefore, the [transcendental] idea [of God] is valid only in relation to the employment of our reason *in reference to the world*. If we were to treat the object of this idea as objectively real, we would then be forgetting that we are thinking of a being in idea only; and in thus beginning from a foundation that is not identifiable on the basis of observation, we would no longer be in a position to apply the principle in a way that is appropriate to the empirical employment of reason . . . .

195

Morality and Metaphysics[1]

Freedom, Immortality, and God[2]

Reason is impelled by its own nature to go beyond the field of experience and, by means of [speculative] ideas alone, to stretch the limits of knowledge to the utmost and not to be satisfied until it has organized its judgments into a self-subsistent systematic whole. Is this systematizing effort a product only of the theoretical interests of reason? Or does it actually arise from reason's *practical* interests . . .?

Theoretical reasoning is transcendentally focused on three subjects: (1) the freedom of the will, (2) the immortality of the soul, and (3) the existence of God . . . . [From a strictly theoretical point of view, it really doesn't matter what is true or false on these three issues because whether the will is free or not, or whether there is an immortal soul or not, or whether God actually exists or not has no bearing on the scientific study of nature.]

In the first place, if the will is free, this refers only to the intelligible cause of our choices. With regard to the phenomenal or outward expressions of the will -- that is, our actions -- [science] must account for them . . . in the same way in which all other phenomena are scientifically explained, namely, in accordance with the unchangeable laws of nature.

---

[1]From Sections 1, 2, and 3 of "The Canon of Pure Reason," B 823-858, which is Chapter II of "II. Transcendental Doctrine of Method."

[2]B 825-829.

196

In the second place, if we could know that the soul has a spiritual nature and is immortal, we could make no use of such knowledge in explaining either the phenomena of this present life or the specific nature of a future state. Our notions of non-material [spiritual] natures are merely negative [spirits are not bodies, not material things, etc.], and such notions do not add anything to our knowledge. Inferences based on such notions are merely fictitious and cannot be approved by philosophy.

If, in the third place, the existence of a supreme intelligence could be proved, this might indeed account, in a general way, for the apparently purposive and orderly constitution of the world; but, even so, we wouldn't be justified in deducing from it any particular arrangement or disposition of things, nor could we infer any such purposive order in situations where it is not perceived. For it is a necessary rule of theoretical [scientific] reason that we must never ignore natural causes or fail to heed the teaching of experience in favor of deducing what we perceive and know from something that completely transcends our knowledge.

In short, these three propositions [concerning freedom, immortality, and God] are, for theoretical [scientific] reason, always transcendent and are entirely useless in the explanation of natural phenomena . . . .

If, then, these three cardinal propositions are not in any way necessary for *knowledge* [that is, science], and if reason nonetheless strongly pushes us to accept them, it would seem that their real value and importance are related to our *practical* and not to our theoretical interests . . . .

All the powers of reason in the field of "pure philosophy" [metaphysics] are concentrated exclusively on the three above-mentioned problems. However, these problems, in turn, direct us to

197

a still higher question: *"What ought we to do*, if the will is free and if there is a God and a future life?" Since this question relates to the highest aim of human existence, it is evident that the ultimate intention of nature in wisely providing us with our well-constituted powers of reason was directed to moral interests alone . . . .

The problem of metaphysical freedom[1]

A will that is governed by the compulsions of physical impulses and instincts is simply an *animal will (arbitrium brutum)* [that is, not free]. A will that is determined independently of physical impulses and instincts by motives based only on reason is a *free will (arbitrium liberum)*, and everything that is related to this will, whether as cause or as consequence, is called *practical* [that is, having to do with action].

[The reality of] practical freedom can be proved through experience. The human will is not governed completely by whatever stimulates or directly affects the senses. We have the power to [resist and] overcome the impressions that arouse our sensuous desires by calling up thoughts of what, in the long run, is useful or hurtful to us. Now, these considerations of what is desirable in relation to our whole existence, that is, of what is really good and useful for us, are based entirely on reason. Reason, therefore, gives us laws that are imperatives, that is, *objective laws of freedom*, which tell us *what ought to happen* (although perhaps it never does happen), thus differing from *laws of nature*, which relate only to *that*

---

[1]B 830-832.

198

which does happen. Thus, we will consider these laws of freedom to be *practical* laws.[1]

Now, it is possible that reason itself (and its prescription of laws of human conduct) is governed by other forces [for example, heredity and environment] and that our apparent freedom from sensuous impulses and instincts is actually determined by natural causes that are higher and more remote than reason. This, however, is a merely theoretical issue that does not concern us from a practical point of view. All we want from reason with regard to human action is a *rule of conduct* that tells what ought or ought not to be done. Thus, we know, on the basis of experience, that freedom of action is one of the causes in nature in the sense that a free will is determined only by the causal power of reason. However, the transcendental [that is, metaphysical] idea of freedom demands that reason (as the determinant of a free will) be itself free from and independent of all determining causes in the world of nature. Transcendental freedom, then, seems to be contrary to the law[s] of nature and to stand beyond all possible experience. Thus, [the idea of transcendental freedom] remains [theoretically] problematic.

But this [theoretical] problem [of transcendental freedom] is not an issue for *practical reason* [that is, reasoning about human action] . . . . [After the issue of practical freedom has been addressed,] there remain only two [further] questions that are of interest in the practical employment of pure reason: (1) Is there a God?, and (2) Is there a future life [that is, a life of the soul beyond death]? The nature and status of transcendental freedom is of

---

[1] A free will, then, is not *un*determined or *un*governed. It is not determined or governed by impulse, instinct, or sensuous desire; but it *is* determined and governed by reason and its practical-moral laws.

199

theoretical interest only. When we are focusing on practical issues related to human action, we can leave the theoretical question of freedom aside as being an issue with which we have no concern . . . . [1]

The existence of moral law[2]

The whole interest of reason, theoretical as well as practical, is concentrated on the three following questions: (1) What can I know?; (2) What ought I to do?; and (3) What may I hope?

The first question [What can I know?] is purely theoretical. I flatter myself in thinking that we have exhausted all the possible answers to this question and have at last found the answer with which reason must be content and with which it is justified in being content, so long as it pays no attention to practical issues. However, we remain just as far from reaching the two great ends to which the whole effort of pure reason is really directed as if, through love of leisure, we had, from the start, refused to take on this intellectual labor. Thus, as far as knowledge is concerned, this, if nothing else, is certain and conclusively established: the knowledge that would enable us to solve these two problems is unattainable by us.

The second question [What ought I to do?] is purely practical. As such, it can be brought under the scope of pure reason; however,

---

[1]While the question of transcendental freedom is of no concern in the context of practical reason, it is a central problem for theoretical reason, and Kant addresses it at length in his discussion of "The Antinomy of Pure Reason," B 435-595 (see especially B 472-479).

[2]B 833-836.

200

it is not a transcendental but a moral issue. Thus, it is not, in itself, a proper subject for coverage in this Critique.[1]

The third question -- If I do what I ought to do, what may I then hope for? -- is both practical and theoretical . . . . [A]ll hoping is directed to happiness, and . . . happiness is the satisfaction of all our desires: *extensively*, with respect to their multiplicity; *intensively*, with respect to their degree; and *protensively*, with respect to their duration. I consider the practical law derived from the motive of *happiness* to be a *pragmatic law* (or prudential rule); whereas, the law (if there is any such law) that has no motive other than *worthiness of being happy* should be thought of as the *moral law*. The *pragmatic law* shows what we have to do in order to become happy; the *moral law* reveals how we must live in order to *deserve* happiness. The *pragmatic law* has an empirical foundation. for it is only through experience that I can learn what my desires are and by what natural means they can be satisfied. The *moral law* takes no account of desires or how they might be satisfied; it considers only the freedom of a rational being in general and the necessary conditions under which alone this freedom can harmonize with a distribution of happiness that is made in accordance with [moral] principles. This moral law can therefore be based on mere ideas of pure reason and be known *a priori*.

I assume that there really exist pure moral laws that determine on a totally *a priori* basis (without regard to empirical motives, that is, to happiness) what is and is not to be done. Such moral laws

---

[1]Kant's answer to the question, "What ought I to do?," is given in three works: *Foundations of the Metaphysics of Morals* (1785); *Critique of Practical Reason* (1788); and *Introduction to the Metaphysics of Morals* (1797).

govern the use that a rational being makes of its freedom. These moral laws command in an *absolute* manner (not merely hypothetically on the supposition of other empirical ends[1]) and are therefore in every respect necessarily binding. I feel justified in making these assumptions because I am supported, not only by the arguments of the most enlightened moralists, but also by the moral judgment of every man in so far as he tries to think about the moral law clearly.

Pure reason, then, contains, not on the theoretical level, but in its practical (that is, moral) expression, principles making possible the experience of such actions as, in accordance with ethical rules, *might* be met with in the history of mankind. For since reason commands that such actions *should* take place, it must be *possible* for them to take place.[2] Thus, a special kind of systematic unity -- that is, the moral unity [of our experience] -- must be possible.

We have indeed found that the systematic unity of nature cannot be proved scientifically (that is, through pure theoretical reason). Although human reason is a causal force in the direction of human freedom in general, it does not have causal efficacy with respect to nature as a whole; and while moral principles proposed by

---

[1]In his later works on ethics (see previous footnote), Kant distinguishes between "hypothetical imperatives" and "categorical imperatives." An *hypothetical imperative* is a command that is conditional on personal motive or desire, for example, "*If* you wish to have a good reputation, be honest." A *categorical imperative* is an unconditional and absolute moral law that applies to all rational beings and is independent of all personal motives or desires, for example, "Be honest" (regardless of consequences).

[2]"Ought" implies "can."

202

reason can indeed give rise to free actions, they cannot give rise to laws of nature. Accordingly, it is in their practical -- that is, in their moral -- expression that the principles of pure reason have objective reality (*objektive Realität*).

The idea of a moral world: morality and happiness[1]

To the extent that the world operates in accordance with moral laws -- which, through the freedom of rational beings, it *can* do and which, according to the necessary laws of morality, it *ought* to do -- to that extent, it is a *moral world*. Such a world is only an intelligible [that is, ideal] world because we are at this point ignoring all the conditions . . . and all the hindrances to which morality is subjected (such as the weakness or depravity of human nature). To this extent, therefore, [the idea of a moral world] is a mere idea, but it is also, at the same time, a practical idea, which really can and ought to have an influence upon the sensible world, an influence that brings that world as far as possible into conformity with the idea. The idea of a moral world thus has objective reality (*objektive Realität*). This does not mean that the moral world is an object of an intellectual [that is non-empirical] intuition (since we are utterly incapable of apprehending any such objects). No, the idea of the moral world refers to the sensible world, but it portrays that world as an object of pure reason in its practical expression, that is, as a *corpus mysticum* [mystical body or community] of [all] the rational beings in it in so far as the free will of each such being is subject to the moral law and thus in complete systematic unity with itself and with the freedom of every other.

---

[1] B 836-837.

203

This is the answer to the first of the two questions that interest pure reason at the practical level [What ought I to do?]: The answer is, *Do that through which you become worthy of happiness.* The second question is: If I live so as not to be unworthy of happiness, may I hope thereby to attain happiness? In answering this question, we must consider whether the principles of pure reason, which decree the moral law *a priori*, also connect the hope [for happiness] necessarily to it.

I maintain that, just as moral principles are necessary to reason at the *practical* level, it is no less necessary at the *theoretical* level to assume that everyone has a real basis to hope for happiness to the extent that he has, by his conduct, made himself worthy of it and that the system of morality is therefore inseparably (though only as an *idea* of pure reason) linked to happiness.

The moral demand for God and life after death[1]

Now, in an ideal world (that is, in a moral world) -- in which we are recognizing no hindrances to morality (such as the desires) -- a system in which happiness is tied and proportioned to morality would be necessary because freedom, partly energized and partly restrained by the moral law, would itself be the cause of general happiness; in such a system, [free and] rational beings, acting in accordance with the principles of the moral law, would themselves be the authors both of their own enduring well-being and of that of others. Of course, such a system of self-rewarding morality is only an idea. To make it actual, *everyone* would have to do what he ought to do, that is, all the actions of rational beings would have to take place just as if they had issued forth from a supreme will that

_____

[1]B 837-841.

204

contains in or under itself all individual wills. But since the moral law is binding on everyone in the use of his freedom, even if others do not act in conformity with the law, neither the way things are in the world nor the causal relations between actions and morality show us how the consequences of these actions are related to happiness. The alleged necessary connection of the hope of happiness with the necessary effort to make the self worthy of happiness cannot therefore be *known* through reason. We can count on it only if a *Supreme Reason* that governs according to moral principles is postulated as the underlying cause of nature.

The idea of such a supreme intelligence in which the most perfect moral will, united with supreme blessedness, is the cause of all happiness in the world insofar as happiness stands in exact proportion to morality, that is, with worthiness to be happy -- this idea I call the *ideal of the supreme good*. It is . . . only in the ideal of the supreme *original* good that pure reason can find the ground of this connection [between morality and happiness], a connection that is necessary from the practical-moral point of view -- and this [God as the Supreme Good] is the foundation of an ideal moral world. Now, we are compelled by reason to see ourselves as members of such a world even though our senses reveal to us nothing but a world of appearances. We must, therefore, assume that our entry into that moral world is a *consequence* of our conduct in the empirical world (where we find no necessary connection between moral worthiness and happiness) and that the ideal moral world we have been considering is, for us, a *future world*. Thus, it follows that [the existence of] God and [the reality of] a future life are two postulates, which, according to the principles of pure reason, are inseparable from the obligation that pure reason itself imposes upon us.

Morality, by itself, constitutes a system. Happiness, however, does not do so unless it is distributed in exact proportion to morality. But this is possible only in an ideal moral world, under a wise author and ruler. Reason is forced to assume the existence of such a ruler, together with life in such a world (which we must regard as a future world). *Otherwise, we would have to regard all moral laws as empty figments of the imagination since without this postulate [of God and a future life] the necessary connection reason claims between these moral laws and happiness could not follow.*[1] Furthermore, everyone regards the moral laws as *commands*; and this the moral laws could not be if they did not, *a priori*, connect suitable consequences with their rules and thus carry with them *promises* and *threats*. But this again they could not do if they did not reside in a necessary being, which, as the supreme good, can alone make such a purposive unity possible.

Leibniz called the world the *kingdom of grace* in so far as we take into account only the rational beings in it and their relations under moral laws and the government of the supreme good. He distinguished this from the *kingdom of nature*, in which these rational beings are indeed subject to moral laws but expect nothing from their actions other than what follows in accordance with the course of nature in the empirical world. We must, therefore, view ourselves in the world of grace, where all happiness awaits us (except to the extent that we limit our share in it through being unworthy of happiness) -- this is a necessary idea of practical reason . . . .

The whole course of our life must be subject to moral maxims; but this is impossible unless reason establishes a connection between

---

[1]The italicized passage is loosely translated. The passage in the German text reads, "*oder die moralischen Gesetze als leere Hirngespinste anzusehen, weil der notwendige Erfolg derselben, den dieselbe Vernunft mit ihnen verknüpft, ohne jene Voraussetzung wegfallen müßte*" (B 839).

the moral law (a mere idea) and a cause that guarantees that moral conduct will have an outcome, either in this or in a future life, that is in exact conformity with our highest aims. Thus, without a God and without a future life, invisible to us now but hoped for, the glorious ideals of morality are indeed objects of approval and admiration, but they are not motivating sources of purpose and action. For [the ideals of morality] do not fulfil all the aspirations that are natural to every rational being and that are determined *a priori* and rendered necessary by pure reason.

Happiness without morality, and morality without happiness[1]

From the standpoint of reason, happiness by itself is not the complete good. Reason cannot approve happiness . . . unless it is united with *worthiness to be happy* (that is, with perfect moral conduct). But, also, morality by itself -- the mere *worthiness* to be happy -- is far from being the complete good. To make the good complete, he who behaves in such a manner as to be worthy of happiness must be able to hope that he will actually achieve happiness. Even a reason that is free from all private purposes and that puts itself in the place of a being that must distribute all happiness to others cannot judge otherwise; for in the practical idea [of the complete good], both elements [happiness and worthiness for happiness] are fundamentally connected, but in such a manner that it is the moral disposition which conditions and makes possible participation in happiness and not conversely the prospect of happiness that makes possible the moral disposition. For then the disposition would not be moral and would therefore not be worthy of complete happiness -- a happiness that, from the standpoint of

---

[1]B 841-842.

reason, has no limitation except that which arises from our own immoral conduct.

What, then, is the supreme good of the moral world that a pure but practical reason commands us to occupy? It is happiness in exact proportion to the moral worth of the rational beings who populate that world. This moral world is, we admit, an ideal world only; the empirical world holds out no promise that any such systematic unity of [moral worth and happiness] can arise from the nature of things. Belief in the reality of this unity is based on nothing but the postulate of a supreme original good [God]. In such a supreme good, self-subsistent reason, equipped with all the power of a supreme cause, sets up, maintains, and completes the universal order of things in accordance with the most perfect design -- an order which in the world of phenomena is largely concealed from us.

A morality-based theology[1]

This morally-grounded view of God has a singular advantage over purely theoretical theology in the sense that it leads us inevitably to the idea of a *single, all-perfect*, and *rational* First Cause. Theoretical theology gives us no objective grounds for such an idea, nor can it give us any conviction as to the existence of such a God. Neither transcendental nor natural theology, no matter how far reason may carry us in those fields, gives us any firm basis for postulating the primordial existence of only some one single being as the original First Cause upon which all natural causes are in all respects dependent. However, if we begin with moral unity as a necessary law of the universe and think out what is necessary to make this law effective and thus an obligatory force for us, we arrive

---

[1]B 842-847.

208

at the conclusion that there must be *one single supreme will* that encompasses all these laws (*der alle diese Gesetze*) in itself. How could there be a complete unity of ends if there were many different [foundational] wills? [Furthermore,] this Divine Being must be *omnipotent* so that the whole of nature and its relation to morality in the world may be subject to His will; He must be *omniscient* so that He may know our innermost sentiments and their moral worth; He must be *omnipresent* so that He may be immediately at hand for the satisfying of every need which the highest good demands; He must be *eternal* so that this harmony of nature and freedom may never fail; and so on . . . .

But when practical reason has risen to the idea of a single primordial being as the supreme good, it must not presume to think that it has transcended the empirical restrictions on its application and has attained to an immediate knowledge of new objects. It cannot start from this idea of God as the supreme good and then simply deduce from it the moral laws themselves. For it is the moral laws that have led us by means of their *inner* practical necessity to postulate the existence of a self-sufficient cause and wise ruler of the universe Who can make the laws effective. We may not, therefore, reverse the procedure and regard the moral laws as accidental and as derived from the mere will of the ruler, especially as we have no conception of such a will except as formed in accordance with these laws.

So far, then, as practical reason has the right to serve as our guide, we shall not look upon actions as obligatory because they are the commands of God, but rather shall view them as divine commands because we have an inward obligation to perform them. We shall study freedom according to the purposive unity that is determined in accordance with the principles of reason; we shall believe ourselves to be acting in conformity with the divine will only in so far as we hold sacred the moral law that reason teaches us from the nature of the actions themselves; and we shall believe that we can serve that will only by furthering what is best in the world, both in ourselves and in others.

Our morality-based theology is thus of immanent use only. It enables us to fulfil our vocation in this present world by showing us how to adapt ourselves to the system of all ends and by warning us against the fanaticism -- and, indeed, the impiety -- of abandoning the guidance of a morally legislative reason in the right conduct of our lives in order to derive guidance directly from the idea of the Supreme Being. For we should then be making a transcendent employment of moral theology; and that, like a transcendent use of pure theoretical thought, will pervert and frustrate the ultimate purposes of reason . . . .

Conclusions on God and immortality[1]

Now, we must admit that the belief in the existence of God is a *doctrinal belief* (*doktrinalen Glauben*).[2] Theoretical knowledge of the world in no way requires us to presuppose the existence of God as the condition of explaining the phenomena exhibited by the world. On the contrary, scientific reason insists that I employ my reason as if everything were nothing but nature. However, the purposive unity of the world is so important a condition of the application of reason to nature that I cannot ignore it, especially since experience provides

---

[1]B 854-858.

[2]Kant defines a "doctrinal belief" as more than a mere opinion, a belief with good evidence or reasons backing it up "although there are as yet no existing means of arriving at certainty in the matter." He mentions his "strong belief" that there are inhabited planets other than the earth as an example of a "doctrinal belief." See B 853.

210

me with so many examples of it. But I can see no way in which this unity can guide my investigation of nature except on the postulate that a supreme intelligence [God] has ordered all things in accordance with the wisest ends. Thus, in order to . . . have guidance in the investigation of nature, we must postulate [the existence of] a wise author of the universe.

Moreover, since the success of my efforts to explain nature this way so clearly confirms the usefulness of this postulate, and since nothing really decisive can be brought against it, I would be saying much too little if I were to declare that I hold the postulate merely as an opinion. Thus, even in this theoretical context, it may be said that I firmly believe in [the reality of] God.

This belief is not, therefore, strictly speaking, practical. It must be entitled a *doctrinal* belief to which the *theology* of nature (physico-theology) must always necessarily give rise. In view of the magnificent equipment of our human nature and the shortness of life, so ill-suited to the full exercise of our powers, we can find in this same divine wisdom a no less sufficient ground for a *doctrinal belief* in the future life of the human soul . . . .

But a merely *doctrinal belief* is rather unstable; we often lose hold of it owing to the theoretical objections against it we frequently encounter, even though in the end we always inevitably return to it.

It is quite otherwise with *moral belief*. For here it is absolutely necessary that something must happen, namely, that I must in all points conform to the moral law. The end is here indisputably established and, as far as I can see, there is only one way in which that end can connect with all other ends and thereby have practical validity, namely, that there be a God and a future world. I also know with complete certainty that no one can be acquainted with any other conditions which lead to the same unity of

211

ends under the moral law. Since, therefore, reason requires me to acknowledge and live by the moral law, I inevitably believe in the existence of God and in [the reality of] a future life. I am certain that nothing can shake this belief since, in that event, my moral principles themselves would be overthrown, and I cannot disclaim them without becoming detestable in my own eyes.

Thus even after reason has failed in all its ambitious attempts to pass beyond the limits of experience, there is still enough left to satisfy us from our practical standpoint. No one, indeed, will be able to boast that he *knows* that there is a God and a future life; if he knows this, then he is the very man for whom I have so long and so vainly sought. All knowledge, if it concerns an object of mere reason, can be communicated; and I might therefore hope that under his instruction my own knowledge would be extended in this wonderful fashion. No, my certainty on these matters is not *logical* but *moral*; and since it rests on subjective grounds (of moral sentiment), I must not even say, "*It is* morally certain that there is a God, etc.," but rather "*I am* morally certain, etc." In other words, belief in a God and in another world [to come] is so interwoven with my moral sentiments that, as there is little danger of my losing the latter, there is equally little cause for fear that the former can ever be taken from me.

The only point that may seem questionable at this point is my basing this rational belief on my moral sentiments. If we leave these aside and take a man who is completely indifferent with regard to moral principles, the question propounded by reason then becomes merely a problem for speculation and can, indeed, be supported by strong grounds of analogy, but not by such as must compel the most stubborn skepticism to give way . . . . But in these questions no man is free from all interest. For although, through lack of good sentiments, a man may have no moral interest, still even in this case enough remains to make him *fear* the existence of a God and a future life. Nothing more is required for this than that he at least cannot pretend that there is any *certainty* that there is *no* such being and *no* such life. Since that would have to be proved by mere reason, and also with certainty, he would have to prove the impossibility of both, which assuredly no one can do. This may therefore serve as *negative* belief, which may not, indeed, give rise to morality and good sentiments, but may nonetheless give rise to an analog of these, namely, a powerful check upon the outbreak of evil sentiments.

But, it will be asked, is this all that pure reason achieves in opening up prospects beyond the limits of experience? Nothing more than two articles of belief? Surely the common understanding could have achieved as much without appealing to philosophers for counsel in the matter . . . .

But I may at once reply: Do you really require that a mode of knowledge that concerns all men should transcend the common understanding and should only be revealed to you by philosophers? Precisely what you find fault with is the best confirmation of the correctness of the above assertions. For we have thereby had revealed to us what we could not have at the start foreseen, namely, that in matters which concern all men without distinction nature is not guilty of any partial distribution of her gifts and that, in regard to the essential ends of human nature, the highest philosophy cannot advance farther than is possible under the guidance which nature has given to even the most ordinary understanding.

JEAN-PAUL SARTRE
(1905-1980 AD)

from

WHAT IS EXISTENTIALISM?[1]

"Existence" is Prior to "Essence"

. . . [B]y existentialism we mean a philosophy that makes human life possible and, in addition, declares that every truth and every action implies a human setting and a human subjectivity [or consciousness] . . . . [More precisely, the existentialists[2]] think that [with regard to human beings] *existence precedes essence* or . . . that subjectivity [rather than objectivity] must be the starting point [in the project of understanding human existence].

Just what does that mean? Let's consider some object that is manufactured, for example, a book or a paper-cutter. Here is an

---

[1]Translated, paraphrased, and edited by George Cronk. © 1996. Translated from Jean-Paul Sartre, *L'Existentialisme est une humanisme* (Paris-VIe: Les Éditions Nagel, 1965). For a standard translation, see Jean-Paul Sartre, ***Existentialism and Human Emotions***, trans. Bernard Frechtman (New York: Philosophical Library, 1957).

[2]Sartre notes that there are both theistic and atheistic existentialists, those who believe in the existence of God and those who don't. Sartre is an atheistic existentialist.

object . . . made by a craftsman whose inspiration came from a concept. He referred to the concept of what a paper-cutter is and likewise to a known method of production, which is part of the concept, something that is, by and large, a routine. Thus, the paper-cutter is an object produced in a certain way and, at the same time, one having a specific use. We cannot imagine a person who produces a paper-cutter but does not know what it is used for. Therefore, with regard to the paper-cutter, we can say that its *essence* -- that is, the . . . production routines and the properties which enable it to be both produced and defined -- precedes its *existence*. Thus, the presence of the paper-cutter or book in front of me is caused by techniques of production, giving us a technological view of the world . . . in which production precedes existence.

When we think of God as the Creator, He is generally thought of as a superior sort of craftsman . . . . [It is widely agreed among philosophers (such as Descartes or Leibniz)] that [the] will more or less follows understanding or at least accompanies it and that when God creates He knows exactly what He is creating. Thus, the concept of a human being in the mind of God can be compared to the concept of a paper-cutter in the mind of the manufacturer. Following certain techniques and a concept, God produces a human being, just as the craftsman, following a definition and a technique, makes a paper-cutter. Thus, the individual human being is the realization of a concept [or essence] in the divine mind.

In the eighteenth century [during the Enlightenment], the . . . *philosophes* discarded the idea of God, but they did not discard the notion that [even on the human level] essence precedes existence. Numerous Enlightenment thinkers such as Diderot, Voltaire, and Kant claimed that there is a *human nature*. This human nature, which is the concept of the human, is found in all human beings, which means that each individual human being is a particular example of a universal concept, that is, *human nature* . . . . So here, too, the *essence* of the human precedes the actual historical *existence* [of human beings] that we find in nature.

Atheistic existentialism, which I represent, is more coherent [than 18th century Enlightenment thought]. It states that if God does not exist, there is at least one being in whom existence precedes essence, a being who exists before he can be defined by any concept. This being is *man* [that is, the *human individual*], or, as Heidegger says, *human reality*. What is meant here by saying that existence precedes essence? It means that, first of all, the human individual exists, turns up, appears in the world, and, only afterwards, defines himself. If the human individual, as the existentialist thinks of him, is indefinable, it is because at first he is *nothing*. Only afterward will he be *something*, and he himself will have made what he will be. Thus, there is no human nature, since there is no God to conceive of it. Not only is the human individual what he conceives himself to be, but he is also only what he wills himself to be after this thrust toward existence.

Self-Creation and Personal Responsibility

The human individual is nothing but what he makes of himself. Such is *the first principle of existentialism* .... [W]hat do we mean by this? Only that the human individual has more dignity than a stone or a table. For we mean that the human individual ... exists ... as the being who hurls himself toward a future and who is conscious of throwing himself into the future. The human individual is ... *a project with subjectivity, a plan that is aware of itself*. A human being is much more than a patch of moss, a piece of garbage, or a cauliflower. Nothing exists prior to this project; there is nothing in heaven; the human individual will be what he will have planned to be. But not [necessarily] what he will *want* to be because by the word "want" we generally mean a conscious decision, which is subsequent to what we have already made of ourselves. I may *want* to belong to a political party, write a book, get married; but all that is only a manifestation of an earlier, more spontaneous choice that is called "will."

But if [human existence] really does precede [human] essence, then the human individual is responsible for what he is [or what he has become]. Existentialism's first move is to make every human being aware of what he is and to make the full responsibility of his existence rest on him. And when we say that a person is responsible for himself, we do not only mean that he is responsible for his own individuality, but that he is responsible for all other human beings.

[Existentialism is often criticized for being a form of *subjectivism*.] Now, the word subjectivism has two meanings . . . . Subjectivism means, on the one hand, that an individual chooses and makes himself; and, on the other, that it is impossible for a person to get beyond his own subjectivity. Existentialism subscribes to the [first[1]] type of subjectivism. When we say that the human individual chooses his own self, we mean that every one of us does this; but we also mean . . . that, in making this choice, the individual also chooses [for] all human beings. In fact, in creating the person that we want to be, there is not a single one of our acts that does not at the same time create an image of humanity as we think it ought to be. To choose to be this or that is to affirm at the same time the value of what we choose. For we can never choose evil. We always choose the good, and nothing can be good for us without being good for all.

---

[1]Sartre writes that existentialism embraces the *second* type of subjectivism: "*C'est le second sens qui est le sens profond de l'existentialisme.*" But that seems inconsistent with what he goes on to say in the following paragraphs. I am therefore assuming that the word "second" is either a mistake on Sartre's part or a misprint.

However, if existence precedes essence, and if we grant that we exist and fashion our image at one and the same time, the image is valid for everybody and for our entire epoch. Thus, our responsibility is much greater than we might have thought because it involves all humankind. If I am a worker and choose to join a Christian trade union rather than be a communist, and if by being a member I want to show that the best thing for humanity is resignation, that the kingdom of man is not of this world, I am not only involving my own case -- I want to be resigned for everyone. As a result, my action has involved all humanity. To take a more individual matter, suppose I want to marry, to have children. Even if this marriage depends solely on my own circumstances or passion or desire, I am committing not only myself but all humanity to monogamy. Therefore, I am responsible for myself and for everyone else. I am creating a certain image of the human through my own choosing. In choosing myself, I choose humanity.

Anguish, Forlornness, and Despair

This helps us understand what is meant by . . . [the existentialist emphasis on] anguish (*angoisse*), forlornness (*délaissement*), and despair (*désespoir*). As you will see, it's all quite simple.

Existential anguish

First, what do we mean by *anguish*? The existentialists say . . . that man is anguish. This means that the man who involves himself and who realizes that he is not only the person he chooses to be, but also a lawmaker who is, at the same time, choosing all humankind as well as himself, cannot escape the feeling of his total and deep responsibility.

Of course, there are many people who do not seem anguished; but we claim that they are hiding their anguish, that they are fleeing from it. Certainly, many people believe that when they do something

219

they themselves are the only ones involved. And when someone says to them, "What if everyone acted that way?," they shrug their shoulders and answer, "But everyone *doesn't* act that way." But really, one should always ask oneself, "What would happen if everybody looked at things that way?" There is no escaping this disturbing thought except by a kind of self-deception (*mauvais foi*, that is, "bad faith"). A man who lies and makes excuses for himself by saying "not everybody does that" is someone whose conscience is ill at ease because the act of lying implies that a universal value is given to the lie.

Anguish is evident even when it conceals itself. This is the anguish that Kierkegaard called the anguish of Abraham. You know the story. An angel has ordered Abraham to sacrifice his son [Isaac]. If it really were an angel [sent by God] who has come and said, "You are Abraham, and you shall sacrifice your son," everything would be all right. But we might first wonder, "Is it really an angel, and am I really Abraham? What proof do I have?"

There was a madwoman who had hallucinations. Someone used to speak to her on the telephone and give her orders. Her doctor asked her, "Who is it who talks to you?" She answered, "He says it's God." What proof did she really have that it was God? If an angel comes to me, what proof is there that it's an angel? And if I hear voices, what proof is there that they come from heaven and not from hell, or from the subconscious, or from a pathological condition? What proves that they are addressed to me?

[By the same token,] what proof is there that I have been appointed to impose my choice and my conception of humanity on the human race? I'll never find any proof or sign to convince me of that. If a voice addresses me, it is always for me to decide that this is "the angel's voice." If I consider that such an action is a good one, it is I who will choose to say that it is good rather than bad.

220

Now, I'm not being singled out as an Abraham, and yet at every moment I'm obliged to perform exemplary acts. For every human being, everything happens as if all humankind had its eyes fixed on him and were guiding itself by what he does. Therefore, everyone should ask himself, "Am I really the kind of person who has the right to act in such a way that humanity might guide itself by my actions?" If he does not say that to himself, then he is masking his anguish.

This is not the kind of anguish that would lead to us retreat from the world, to inaction or quietism. It is a simple sort of anguish that everybody who has had responsibilities is familiar with. For example, when a military officer takes the responsibility for an attack and sends a certain number of men to death, he chooses to do so, and in the main he alone makes the choice. No doubt, his orders come from above, but they are often quite broad. He interprets them, and on this interpretation depend the lives of ten or fourteen or twenty men. In making a decision he cannot help having a certain anguish. All leaders know this anguish. That doesn't keep them from acting. On the contrary, it is the very condition of their action. For it implies that they foresee a number of possibilities, and when they choose one, they realize that it has value only because it is chosen. We shall see that this kind of anguish, which is the kind that existentialism describes, is explained . . . by a direct responsibility to the other men whom it involves. It is not a curtain separating us from action, but it is part of action itself.

Existential forlornness

When we speak of *forlornness*, a term Heidegger liked, we mean only that God does not exist and that we have to face all the

221

consequences of this.[1] The existentialist is strongly opposed to a certain kind of secular humanism that would like to abolish God with the least possible expense. In the 1880s, some French professors tried to set up a secular humanism that went something like this: God is a useless and costly hypothesis. We are discarding that hypothesis, but, meanwhile, in order for there to be moral standards, a society, a well-ordered world, it is essential that certain values be taken seriously and that they be considered to have an *a priori* [that is, absolute] existence. It must be obligatory, *a priori*, to be honest, not to lie, not to beat your wife, to have children, etc., etc. So we're going to try a little device that will permit us to show that values exist all the same, inscribed in a heaven of ideas, even though God does not exist. In other words -- and this, I believe, is the tendency of all French radicalism -- nothing will be changed if God does not exist. We shall find ourselves with the same norms of honesty, progress, and humanity, and we shall have made of God an outdated hypothesis that will peacefully die off by itself.

In opposition to this, the existentialist thinks that it is very distressing that God does not exist because all possibility of finding [objective, absolute] values in a heaven of ideas disappears along with Him. There can no longer be an absolute Good since there is no infinite and perfect consciousness to think it. Nowhere is it written that the Good exists, that we must be honest, that we must not lie. The fact is that we are in a universe where there are only human beings.

Dostoyevsky has written, "If God didn't exist, everything would be permitted." That is the point of departure of existentialism. Indeed, everything is permissible if God does not exist, and as a result man is forlorn [that is, abandoned, alone] because neither within him nor

---

[1]Sartre's comments on forlornness are applicable only to atheistic existentialism. He seems at this point to have forgotten the theistic existentialists.

222

without does he find anything [really stable] to cling to. He can't start making excuses for himself. If existence really does precede essence, there is no explaining things away by reference to a given and unchanging human nature. In other words, there is no determinism. Man is free. Man is freedom. If God does not exist, we find no [objective or absolute] values or commands to turn to in order to legitimize our conduct. In the bright realm of values, we have no justifications and no excuses, neither behind us nor before us. We are alone -- with no excuses.

That is the idea I . . . am trying to get across when I say that *the human individual is condemned to be free.* Condemned because he did not create himself [that is, he did not cause his own existence]; yet in other respects he is free. Once thrown into the world, he is responsible for everything he does. The existentialist does not believe in the power of passion [to determine our actions]. He will never agree that a sweeping passion is a ravaging torrent that fatalistically leads a person to certain acts and is therefore an excuse. The existentialist thinks that the human individual is responsible for his passion.

The existentialist does not think that a person is going to help himself by finding in the world some sign by which to guide himself . . . . He will interpret any such sign to suit himself. Therefore, the existentialist thinks that humanity, with no support and no aid, is condemned at every moment to invent humanity. Ponge [a French writer], in a very fine article, has said, "Man is the future of man." That's exactly it. But if this is taken to mean that this future is recorded in heaven, that God sees it, then it is false because it would really no longer be a future. If it is taken to mean that, whatever a person may be, there is a future to be made, a virgin future before him, then this remark is sound. But then we are forlorn [that is, on our own].

To give you an example that will enable you to understand [the condition of] forlornness better, I shall cite the case of one of my

223

students who came to see me under the following circumstances: His father was on bad terms with his mother, and, moreover, was inclined to be a collaborationist.[1] His older brother had been killed in the German offensive of 1940, and the young man, with somewhat immature but generous feelings, wanted to avenge him. His mother lived alone with him, very much upset by the half-treason of her husband and the death of her oldest son. The boy [my student] was her only consolation.

The young man was faced with the choice of leaving for England and joining the Free French Forces -- that is, leaving his mother behind -- or remaining with his mother and helping her to carry on. He was fully aware that the woman lived only for him and that his going away -- and perhaps his death -- would plunge her into [utter] despair. He was also aware that every act that he did for his mother's sake was a sure thing, in the sense that it was [actually] helping her to carry on, whereas every effort he made toward going off and fighting was an uncertain move that might run aground and prove completely useless. For example, on his way to England, he might, while passing through Spain, be detained indefinitely in a Spanish camp; or he might reach England or Algiers and be stuck in an office at a desk job.

As a result, he was faced with two very different kinds of action: one, concrete and immediate, but concerning only one individual [his mother]; the other concerned an incomparably vaster group, a national collectivity, but for that very reason was uncertain and might be interrupted en route. At the same time, he was wavering between two kinds of morality. One the one hand, a morality of sympathy or personal devotion; on the other hand, a broader [social and political]

---

[1]That is, a collaborator with the Germans, who had invaded and occupied France early in World War II.

morality, but one whose success was more doubtful. He had to choose between the two.

Who could help him choose? Christian doctrine? No. Christian doctrine says, "Be charitable, love your neighbor, take the more rugged path, etc., etc." But which is the more rugged path? Whom should he love as a neighbor? The fighting man or his mother? Which does the greatest good, the vague act of fighting in a group, or the concrete one of helping a particular human being to go on living? Who can decide in the abstract? Nobody. No book of ethics can tell him. Kant says, "Never treat any person as a means but only as an end." Very well, if I stay with my mother, I'll treat her as an end and not as a means; but by virtue of this very fact, I'm running the risk of treating the people around me, who are fighting, as means; and, conversely, if I go to join those who are fighting, I'll be treating them as an end, and, by doing that, I run the risk of treating my mother as a means.

If values are vague, and if they are always too broad for the concrete and specific case that we are considering, the only thing left for us is to trust our instincts. That's what this young man tried to do, and when I saw him, he said, "In the end, feeling is what counts. I ought to choose whichever pushes me in a certain direction. If I feel that I love my mother enough to sacrifice everything else for her -- my desire for revenge, for action, for adventure -- then I'll stay with her. If, on the contrary, I feel that my love for my mother isn't enough, I'll leave."

But how can we determine the value of a feeling? What gives his feeling for his mother value? Precisely the fact that he remained with her. I may say that I like so-and-so well enough to sacrifice a certain amount of money for him, but I may say so only if I've done it. I may say "I love my mother well enough to remain with her" if I *have* remained with her. The only way to determine the value of this affection is, precisely, to perform an act that confirms and defines it.

225

But, since I require this affection to justify my act, I find myself caught in a vicious circle.

On the other hand, Gide has well said that a mock feeling and a true feeling are almost indistinguishable. To decide that I love my mother and will remain with her, or to remain with her by putting on an act, amount somewhat to the same thing. In other words, the feeling is constructed by the acts one performs. Therefore, I cannot refer to the feeling in order to be guided by it. Which means that I can neither seek within myself the true condition that will impel me to act, nor can I turn to a system of ethics for concepts that will permit me to act.

You will say, "At least he did go to a teacher for advice." But if you seek advice from a priest . . . , you have chosen this priest; you already knew, more or less, just about what advice he was going to give you. In other words, choosing your advisor is involving yourself. The proof of this is that if you are a Christian, you will say, "Consult a priest." But some priests are collaborating, some are just marking time, some are resisting. Which to choose? If the young man chooses a priest who is resisting or one who is collaborating, he has already decided on the kind of advice he's going to get. Therefore, in coming to see me he knew the answer I was going to give him, and I had only one answer to give: "You're free -- choose, that is, invent." No general ethical theory can show you what is to be done; there are no sure signs in the world. The Catholics will reply, "But there are." Even if I grant this, it is I myself who choose the meaning the signs have.

When I was a prisoner, I knew a rather remarkable young man who was a Jesuit. He had entered the Jesuit order in the following way: He had a number of very bad breaks. When he was a child, his father died, leaving him in poverty, and he was a scholarship student at a religious institution where he was constantly made to feel that he was being kept out of charity. Then he failed to get any of the honors and distinctions that children like. Later on, at about the age of eighteen, he

226

bungled a love affair. Finally, at twenty-two, he failed in military training -- a childish enough matter, but it was the last straw.

This young man might well have felt that he had botched everything. It was a sign of something, but of what? He might have taken refuge in bitterness or despair, but he very wisely looked upon all this as a sign that he was not made for secular triumphs, and that only the triumphs of religion, holiness, and faith were accessible to him. He saw the hand of God in all this, and so he entered the order.

Who can help seeing that he alone decided what the sign meant? Some other interpretation might have been drawn from this series of setbacks, for example, that he might have done better to turn carpenter or revolutionist. So he is fully responsible for the interpretation. Forlornness implies that we ourselves choose our being. Forlornness and anguish go together.

Existential despair

As for *despair*, the term has a very simple meaning. It means that we shall confine ourselves to considering only what depends upon our will, or on the collection of probabilities that make our action possible. When we want something, we always have to consider probabilities. I may be counting on the arrival of a friend. The friend is coming by rail or streetcar. This assumes that the train will arrive on schedule or that the streetcar will not jump the track. I am left in the realm of possibility. But possibilities are to be considered only to the point where my action is consistent with the sum of these possibilities and no further. The moment the possibilities I am considering are not strictly involved in my action, I ought to disengage myself from them because no God, no scheme, can make the world and its possibilities conform to my will. When Descartes said, "Conquer yourself rather than the world," he meant essentially the same thing.

227

The Marxists to whom I have spoken reply, "You can rely on the support of others in your action, which obviously has certain limits because you're not going to live forever. That means rely on both what others are doing elsewhere to help you -- in China, in Russia -- and what they will do later on, after your death, to carry on the action and lead it to its fulfillment, which will be the Revolution. Indeed, you *must* rely on that; otherwise you're immoral." I reply at once that I will always rely on fellow fighters to the extent that these comrades are involved with me in a specific and common struggle, in the unity of a party or a group in which I can more or less make my weight felt; that is, one whose ranks I am in as a fighter and whose movements I am aware of at every moment. In such a situation, relying on the unity and will of the party is exactly like counting on the fact that the train will arrive on time or that the streetcar won't jump the track. But, given that man is free and that there is no human nature for me to depend on, I cannot count on men whom I do not know [just] by relying on human goodness or humanity's concern for the good of society. I don't know what will become of the Russian Revolution; I may hold it up as an example to the extent that at the present time it is apparent that the proletariat [working class] plays a part in Russia that it plays in no other nation. But I can't be sure that this will inevitably lead to a triumph of the proletariat. I've got to limit myself to what I see.

Given that human beings are free and that tomorrow they will freely decide what man will be, I can't be sure that, after my death, my fellow fighters will carry on my work to bring it to its maximum perfection. Tomorrow, after my death, some men may decide to turn to Fascism, and the others may be cowardly or muddled enough to let them do it. Fascism will then be the human reality. So much the worse for us.

A Philosophy of Action

Actually, things will be as humanity will have decided they are to be. Does that mean that I should withdraw from life, retreat into inaction? No. First, I should engage myself; then act on the old saying, "Nothing ventured, nothing gained." Nor does it mean that I shouldn't belong to a [political] party, but rather that I shall have no illusions and shall do what I can. For example, suppose I ask myself, "Will socialism, as such, ever come about?" All I can know is that I'm going to do everything in my power to bring it about. Beyond that, I can't count on anything.

There are people who say, "Let others do what I can't do." Existentialism says the very opposite. It declares, "There is no reality except in action." Moreover, it goes further, since it adds, "Man is nothing but his project; he exists only to the extent that he fulfills himself; he is therefore nothing but the totality of his acts, nothing but his life."

According to this, we can understand why our philosophy horrifies certain people. Quite often, the only way they can bear their misery is to think, "Circumstances have been against me. What I've been and done doesn't show my true worth. To be sure, I've had no great love, no great friendship, but that's because I haven't met a man or woman who was worthy. The books I've written haven't been very good because I haven't had enough time to spend on them. I haven't had children to devote myself to because I didn't find a man with whom I could have spent my life. So there remains within me, unused but quite alive, a host of tendencies, inclinations, and possibilities that one wouldn't infer from the mere series of things I've done."

Now, for the existentialist, there is really no love other than one that manifests itself in a person's being in love. There is no genius other than one that is expressed in works of art. The genius of Proust is the sum of his works; the genius of Racine is his series of tragedies. Outside of that, there is nothing. Why say that Racine could have written another tragedy when he didn't write it?

A man is engaged in life, leaves his mark on it, and outside of that there is nothing. To be sure, this may seem a harsh thought to someone whose life hasn't been a success. But . . . it prompts people to understand that reality alone is what counts, that dreams, expectations, and hopes do no more than to define a man as a disappointed dream, as miscarried hopes, as vain expectations -- in other words, to define him negatively and not positively. However, when we say, "You are nothing but your life," that does not necessarily mean that the artist will be judged solely on the basis of his works of art. A thousand other things will contribute toward defining him. What we mean is that a man is nothing but a series of undertakings, that he is the sum, the organization, the collection of the relationships that make up these undertakings . . . .

In our works of fiction, we write about people who are soft, weak, cowardly, and sometimes even downright bad. Our fiction is often called pessimistic, but not because the characters depicted are soft, weak, cowardly, or bad. If we were to say, as Zola did, that they are that way because of heredity, the workings of the environment, society, or because of biological or psychological determinism, our critics would be reassured and comforted. They would then say, "Well, that's what we're like; no one can do anything about it." But when an existentialist writes about a coward, he says that this coward is responsible for his cowardice. He's not like that because he has a cowardly heart or lung or brain; he's not like that because of his physiological makeup. No, he's like that because he has made himself a coward by his [own] actions. There's no such thing as a cowardly constitution. There are nervous constitutions; there is poor blood, as the common people say; and there are strong constitutions. But the man whose blood is poor is not a coward for that reason. What makes cowardice is the *act* of

230

renouncing or yielding. A [physiological] constitution is not an act. The coward is defined on the basis of the *acts* he performs. People feel, in a vague sort of way, that this coward we're talking about is *guilty* of being a coward, and the thought frightens them. What people would like is for a coward or a hero to be born that way . . . .

That's what people really want to think. If you're born cowardly, you may set your mind perfectly at rest. There's nothing you can do about it. You'll be cowardly all your life, whatever you may do. If you're born a hero, you may set your mind just as much at rest. You'll be a hero all your life. You'll drink like a hero and eat like a hero.

What the existentialist says is that the coward makes himself cowardly, that the hero makes himself heroic. There's always a possibility for the coward not to be cowardly any more and for the hero to stop being heroic. What counts is total involvement. Some one particular action or set of circumstances is not total involvement . . . .

Existential Subjectivity

The Cartesian *cogito*

[Many of our critics charge us] with imprisoning the human individual in his private subjectivity . . . . The subjectivity of the individual is indeed our point of departure, and this for strictly philosophical reasons . . . . There can be no other truth to start off from than this: *I think; therefore, I exist.*[1] There we have the absolute truth

---

[1]Here, Sartre is quoting René Descartes, who is the author of the famous slogan, "*Cogito, ergo sum*," which in Latin means "I think, therefore I am." See Descartes' **Discourse on Method**, Part IV, in **Discourse on Method and**

231

of consciousness becoming aware of itself. Every theory that removes man from the moment in which he becomes aware of himself is, at its very beginning, a theory that hides truth, for outside the Cartesian *cogito*, all views are only probable, and a theory of probability that is not bound to a truth [that is certain] dissolves into thin air. In order to describe the probable, you must have a firm hold on the truth. Before there can be any truth whatsoever, there must be an absolute truth. And this one [the *cogito*] is simple and easily arrived at; it's on everyone's doorstep; it's [just] a matter of grasping it directly.

Also, this theory is the only one that gives the human individual dignity, the only one that does not reduce him to an object. The effect of all [forms of philosophical] materialism is to treat all humans, including the one who is philosophizing, as objects, that is, as a series of determined reactions in no way distinguished from the collection of qualities and phenomena that constitute a table or a chair or a stone. Existentialists definitely wish to establish the human realm as a set of values distinct from the material realm.

Self and others -- intersubjectivity

But the subjectivity that we have thus arrived at, and which we have claimed to be . . . [fundamentally real], is not a strictly individual [or private] subjectivity, for we have shown that one discovers in the *cogito*, not only oneself, but others as well . . . . [T]hrough the *I think*, I reach my own self in the presence of others, and the others are just as real to me as my own self. So one who achieves self-awareness through the *cogito* also discovers all others, and he discovers them as the condition of his own existence. He realizes that he cannot be anything

---

Meditations on First Philosophy, trans. Donald A. Cress (Indianapolis: Hackett Publishing Company, 1980), p. 17.

(in the sense that we say that someone is spiritual or nasty or jealous) unless others recognize it as such. In order to get any truth about myself, I must have contact with the other. The other is indispensable to my own existence, as well as to my knowledge about myself. This being so, in discovering my inner being, I discover the other at the same time, who appears before me as a free being that thinks and wills only for or against me. Hence, let us at once announce the discovery of a world that we shall call *intersubjectivity*. This is the world in which a person decides what he is and what others are.

The human condition

Furthermore, although it is impossible to find in every person some universal essence that would be human nature, yet there does exist a universal *human condition*. It's not by chance that today's thinkers speak more readily of the human condition than of human nature. By *condition* they mean, more or less definitely, the fixed limits that outline humanity's fundamental situation in the universe. Historical situations vary. A person may be born a slave in a pagan society or a feudal lord or a proletarian. What does not vary is the necessity for him (1) to exist in the world, (2) to be at work there, (3) to be there in the midst of other people, and (4) to be mortal there.

These limits are neither subjective nor objective, or, rather, they have an objective *and* a subjective side. Objective because they are to be found everywhere and are recognizable everywhere [that is, they are universal]; subjective because they are *lived* and are nothing if a person does not live them, that is, if he does not freely determine his existence with reference to them. And though the ways in which people respond to the human condition may differ [from time to time, place to place, person to person] . . . , none of these responses is completely strange to me because they all appear as attempts either to pass beyond the limits of the human condition or to recede from them or to deny them or to

233

adapt to them. Consequently, every human situation, no matter how individual it may be, has a universal value . . . .

The Unavoidability of Choice and the Call of Freedom

[W]hat is not possible is not to choose. I can always choose, and I ought to recognize that if I do not choose, I am still choosing . . . . [M]an is an organized project in which he himself is involved. Through his choice, he involves all humankind, and he cannot avoid making a choice: either he will remain unmarried, or he will marry without having children, or he will marry and have children. Anyhow, whatever he may do, it is impossible for him not to take full responsibility for the way he handles his problems . . . . Man makes himself. He isn't completely defined at the start. In choosing his values, he makes himself, and the force of circumstances is such that he cannot abstain from choosing a set of values . . . . Existentialism defines the human situation as involving free choice, with no excuses and no hiding places. Everyone who takes refuge behind the excuse that he is driven by his passions, everyone who sets up any kind of determinism, is dishonest [that is, guilty of *mauvais foi*, bad faith] . . . .

I declare that freedom in every concrete circumstance can have no other aim than to want itself. If a person has once become aware that in his forlornness he creates and imposes values, he can no longer want but one thing, and that is freedom -- freedom as the foundation of all values. That doesn't mean than he wants it in the abstract. It means simply that the ultimate meaning of the acts of honest people is the quest for freedom as such. One who belongs to a communist or revolutionary union wants to reach concrete goals; these goals imply an abstract desire for freedom; but this freedom is wanted in something concrete. We want freedom for freedom's sake and in every particular circumstance. And in wanting freedom, we discover that it depends